Story-Formed Pathways to

Best Practices for Everyday Life

EDITION 2

DALTON REIMER

Copyright © 2023 by Dalton Reimer All rights reserved.

All rights reserved. No part of this book may be reproduced or transmitted in any form or by any means, electronic or mechanical, including photocopying, recording, or by any information storage and retrieval system without express written permission from the author, except in the case of brief quotations embodied in critical reviews and certain other noncommercial uses permitted by copyright law.

Scriptures quotations, unless otherwise noted, are from the Revised Standard Version of the Bible, copyright 1946, 1952, and 1971 the Division of Christian Education of the Natioanl Council of the Churches of Christ in the United States of America. Used by permission. All rights reserved.

Scripture quotations taken from the Revised English Bible, copyright Cambridge University Press and Oxford University Press 1989. All rights reserved.

ISBNs
978-1-64133-886-8 paperback
978-1-64133-887-5 ebook

Printed in the United States of America.
Brilliant Books Literary
137 Forest Park Lane Thomasville
North Carolina 27360 USA

ACCLAIM for Story-Formed Pathways to Peace (First Edition)

Awarded first place – "Best Non-Fiction" – in 2019 Pacific Book Awards

- Pacific Book Review

...a phenomenal book...superbly written: a cogent yet complex journey through Biblical stories in their original context and in modern application.

- John Paul Lederach, Professor Emeritus of International Peacemaking, University of Notre Dame

Story-Formed Pathways to Peace is a wonderful and informative read. So much of our existing literature on conflict and peace studies has taken a turn toward either the abstract conceptual or the purely technical. It is a delight to find an approach that incites the imagination, grounds the conversation in real life stories, and provides such an array of perspectives. Dalton brings his years of experience in practice and teaching into pathways that enlighten and encourage, much needed for the current morass of the unimaginative and unproductive landscape of polarization we seem to inhabit across our globe today. I highly recommend this excellent book.

- Laura N. Goerzen, Mennonite Church Pastor

Dalton Reimer's Story-Formed Pathways to Peace highlights the often missed relational dynamics of familiar stories in Genesis and the Gospels. From the first families in Genesis to Jesus' teachings on families and relationships, Reimer draws out the challenges of living peacefully with one another whether in the intimate setting of the family, or in the broader context of the world community.

Reimer highlights the failures and successes of the biblical families and communities that have gone before us, and then introduces the transformative way of peace taught by Jesus. My congregation loved the worship series I led based on Reimer's work. They appreciated the opportunity to see the interpersonal conflicts of Genesis in new ways that connected them to the sorts of conflicts they encounter in daily life.

- Ron Claassen, Co-Founder and former Director of the Center for Peacemaking and Conflict Studies at Fresno Pacific University

Stories featured in Story-Formed Pathways to Peace as told by Reimer opened each morning of our week-long, 8 hour per day, Basic Institute in Conflict Management, Peacemaking and Restorative Justice that he and I offered annually for 25 years. He presented the stories in a way that students, regardless of their faith or values perspective, listened and eagerly anticipated the next day's story. In their final course reflections, students consistently included how much they learned from them and how these stories provided inspiration and motivation to want to learn more about being a peacemaker. As he prepared and told these stories, he consistently combined his academic excellence with his deep Anabaptist faith (or commitment to peacemaking). Through the years, he added to and further refined them. I also listened and learned from him as he continued to gain new insights. As I read Story-Formed Pathways to Peace, I could hear him telling the stories and thoroughly enjoyed the additional thoughts added in the book that emerged as he was writing. I would strongly recommend this book for everyone who is open to learning about the connection between Genesis, Jesus, and current events. I think that while anyone will benefit from reading it, it will be especially valuable to leaders of faith communities, peacemaking practitioners, and academics who teach peace.

- David Augsburger, Professor Emeritus of Pastoral Care and Counseling, Fuller Theological Seminary

Isak Dinesin wrote "All our sorrows can be borne if we can weave them into a story." Dalton Reimer tells us that our conflicts can be turned toward transformative ends if we are willing to learn from ignored or forgotten stories, YES. Dalton Reimer is a pathfinder. He has been searching for pathways that trace a way through the thickets or lead out of the deserts of conflict. A professor, he knows the literature of peace studies; a dean, he knows the signs of community conflict; a churchman, he has seen the chaos created by people who are troubled by similarities and blame it on their differences. The pathways, he has concluded, are found not in propositions or prohibitions, but in stories. Stories form our best repositories of wisdom. In stories we see people move toward each other again after bitter division. From stories we gain the hope to reach out after lonely alienation. Archetypical stories, from the Hebrew and Christian scriptures, are particularly instructive, illuminating the depths of human rivalry, hostility and brutality. Reimer's half century of exploration of why people hurt each other and how they harm community provides a narrative wisdom beginning with the first sibling murder and stretching to the murder of the ultimate innocent victim. These meditations provide the reader with a depth analysis of how severed limbs of relationships can be restored and embrace the other once more. They teach us how, they teach us to reach out again.

- Kirkus Review

In this cogent book, Reimer's tone is both scholarly and accessible... A thoughtful, well-argued defense of the central role of peacemaking....

DEDICATION

To
Beverly

Our children and grandchildren
Melissa, Tabitha and Ross, Joseph
Julia
Charles and Gina, Joshua, Rachel
and
Parents who have gone before
Siblings who have journeyed alongside
Continuing offspring from generation to generation
As of now including two delightful great-granddaughters, Opal and Airlee

Story-Formed Pathways to PEACE

Best Practices for Everyday Life

CONTENTS

Story-Formed Pathways to Peace
Best Practices for Everyday Life

Preface I
Introduction... III

Part I

Genesis: Beginning Pathways 1
    Chapter 1: Murder: Cain And Abel.................................3
    Chapter 2: Separation: Abraham And Sarah............................20
    Chapter 3: Conciliation: Esau And Jacob 39
    Chapter 4: Genocide: Dinah And Her Brothers 53
    Chapter 5: Reconciliation: Joseph And His Brothers................65

Part II

Jesus: Transformative Pathways...85
    Chapter 6: The View From A Galilean Hillside......................87
    Chapter 7: Transformative Pathways For Families 98
    Chapter 8: Transformative Pathways For Neighbors...............118
    Chapter 9: Transformative Pathways For Enemies.................135

Conclusion..163
Postscript 165
Endnotes 173
About The Author 181

PREFACE

The stories of Genesis and Jesus inform all three of the Abrahamic religions of our world. Genesis is the shared story of creation and earth's first families. Jesus is respected as rabbi and teacher in Judaism, prophet in Islam, and Savior and Lord in Christianity. Both Genesis and Jesus point us beyond the "no" of violence to the "yes" of peace, *shalom* in Hebrew and *salaam* in Arabic. While I write as a Christian, I invite adherents of all three religions, along with those interested in the pursuit of peace for whatever reason, to consider what we might learn from the early family stories of Genesis and the later story and teachings of Jesus, both at points of new beginnings.

My own story leading to this work began in childhood. I am deeply indebted to my parents, who schooled me through both home and church in biblical knowledge and the disciplines of Christian faith. Reading the Bible and praying were daily family practices while growing up.

The specific impetus for this work began in the late 1980s in a weekly Bible study class I taught in my local church. The class was a teacher's delight. Senior citizens all, they were in no hurry to go anywhere. Not only did they give me freedom to choose the topic of study, but they also left the time open ended. So we embarked on an extended study of the stories of brothers, biological and metaphorical, in the Old and New Testaments of the Christian Bible. I am indebted to these Bible study friends. Though I have not followed each of their journeys, I assume by now most, if not all, have reached their eternal destination where peace is surely at home.

This study of the late 1980s evolved in the early 1990s into a series of story-based lectures on conflict and peacemaking in the family stories of Genesis. I have given these lectures many times—from the early 1990s until 2014 as the introduction to each day of an intensive, week-long Basic Institute in Conflict Management and Mediation offered by the Center for Peacemaking and Conflict

Studies of my university, and in other teaching and lecture settings on five different continents. I have learned from the responses of those who have listened. Their affirmations and encouragement to publish have kept me working.

In 1990 the Center for Peacemaking and Conflict Studies at Fresno Pacific University was established. Ron Claassen and I served as co-founding directors. Simultaneously, we began a teaching partnership in the Basic Institute in Conflict Management and Mediation, which we continued until 2014. We have both valued the balance between more story-oriented and topical approaches to learning. I am most grateful to him for providing space for my opening story telling in the Institute past my formal retirement from fulltime teaching and co-directorship of the Center, and for his continuing affirmation and encouragement.

I have dedicated this work to both my immediate and intergenerational families, for whom I am most grateful. My family has been a primary lab for learning. My dedication of this work to them expresses my love and special thanks to these who are closest to me.

Finally, a pathway to publishing has its own story. At the beginning of this journey, Mark Fretz, Publishing Consultant, was a helpful and valuable guide. Along the way, a brief exchange with Stephen Hanselman of LevelFiveMedia, LLC, added further insights. I'm indeed grateful to both for their counsel.

INTRODUCTION

No Google maps or travel guidebooks existed in ancient, preliterate villages. But there were guides for living. Village elders were these guides, and their medium was story. The stories they told constituted the memory of the village—stories of where they came from and the nature of the world they inhabited. Characters in the stories provided both pro-social and anti-social models for living. As villagers saw themselves in the stories, they functioned as mirrors reflecting what behaviors were to be affirmed and also denied. So as memory, models and mirrors, stories shaped the village community. The storytellers themselves served as the library of the village, as Pascal Kulungu, an African friend, once put it, embodying the wisdom of the past for the present and future.

Among those stories preserved for our present global village are the stories of the ancient book of Genesis. From generation to generation these stories have informed adherents of all three of the monotheistic, Abrahamic religions of our world, and inspired others beyond. They continue to do so today as they not only tell us how all began, but also how to find our way to where peace is at home. They are as contemporary today as when they were first told.

Story, moreover, is a universal language. Stories continue to powerfully shape our communities, whether traditional or modern. George Gerbner, American media scholar, observes that "those who tell stories hold the power in society. Today," he continues, "television tells most of the stories to most of the people, most of the time."[1]

Gerbner has it right. Yet even in this age when television has dethroned the traditional storyteller, some older stories just refuse to go away. Among these are the stories of the book of Genesis, along with the story of Jesus.

The Genesis stories were first passed from generation to generation through oral transmission. These stories were ultimately collected and shaped into a single narrative by an editor, likely in the tenth century BCE. As now presented in the unified text that we have inherited, the book opens with an account of creation and early post-Eden generations to the great flood story of Noah and his family. This is followed by the transitional story of Babel and the origins of human diversity. What then follows, occupying the greater portion of Genesis, are the family stories of the three great patriarchs—Abram, renamed Abraham; Isaac; and Jacob, renamed Israel.

Even though these stories are ancient, they still engage us, because they draw on universal human experiences. They are timeless classics, even though we may set them aside for a while. They are always there waiting for our return. So it is that visual artists, novelists, poets, dramatists, musicians, filmmakers and others continue to find inspiration for creativity in these stories. Scholars continue to probe them for new insights. Even television, on occasion, returns for another look, as in the mid-1990s series on Genesis anchored by Bill Moyers of U.S. public television. Noting the interest at the time, *Time* magazine featured the book on the cover of its October 28, 1996, issue. Simultaneously, new translations of the book also appeared.

My interest, which predates this flurry of attention in the mid-1990s, is to examine the post-Eden family stories of Genesis through the lens of conflict, violence and peacemaking, along with the later story of Jesus. In so doing, I follow in the footsteps of Old Testament scholar Phyllis Trible, who has suggested that the Bible is like "a pilgrim wandering through history" to which each age brings its questions.[2] Trible sees hope for finding direction in the merger of past and present, and I concur.

In the Beginning

How do we make peace in a world filled with conflict and violence? That is a dominant question of our time. We may well merge past and present in search of answers, but where do we begin?

Critics of Jesus came to him one day with a moral question pertaining to marital relationships. In response, he pointed them back to the early chapters of Genesis—how it had been in the beginning (Matthew 19:3-12). His assumption was that beginnings serve as points of moral clarity.

While beginnings do not answer all questions, they do serve as points of moral reference and clarity. So in pursuit of answers to our question of peacemaking in a world filled with conflict and violence, we do well also to go back to the beginning.

The story of creation in Genesis is climaxed with the creation of man and woman. Children soon follow. So the first social unit, the family, was established. Here is where life began then, and continues to begin today. And it is in the family that conflict first happens and alternative modes of conflict resolution are learned. Time has not diminished this truth. As psychiatrist James Gilligan has written in our time: "All of our basic problem-solving, problem-exacerbating, and problem-creating strategies, for living and dying, are learned first at home."[3]

I begin then with the question: How was it at the beginning with the family? For the family is not only the beginning context for life; it is also the beginning context for moral clarity. So earth's first families guide us along alternative pathways, for better or worse, for working with conflict and violence. That is Part I of our study.

But there are also second beginnings, and among these are the beginnings of our various religious traditions. These, too, are points of moral clarity, not only for families, but also for neighbors and enemies. In Part II, then, I examine core teachings related to conflict, violence and peacemaking at the genesis of my Christian faith, which I know best. My invitation to Jewish and Islamic readers, along with others, is to reflect comparatively in the same manner on the beginnings of their traditions—the Mosaic and prophetic traditions of Judaism and the Mohammedan and prophetic traditions of Islam, among others.

The Foundation of Freedom

All three of the Abrahamic, monotheistic religions of our world begin with the assumption that as humans we are free to choose our way in the world. From the beginning it has been so.

The Genesis narrative begins with the grand declaration: "In the beginning…God created the heavens and the earth…" With God as the master artist at work, we should expect a masterpiece. And so it was. Seven times during the process of creating, God stepped back to assess the emerging masterpiece and declared it to be good. Indeed, the seventh time as "very good." Goodness, in the Hebrew mind, is found in the number seven, and so seven days of creation and seven declarations of "good" represent a masterpiece of God's making.

Placed into the midst of this remarkable work of creation, nevertheless, was a challenge—the challenge of freedom. In the first real test of freedom posed by a cunning serpent, earth's first two humans miserably failed. Their failure cost them their first home, the lush and verdant Garden of Eden, from which they were banished. For choices also have consequences. This loss set the stage for the remainder of the human story.

Among the many things this first narrative of creation teaches us, then, is the great truth of freedom. God has created us free to choose our way in this world. If that were not so, there would be no point to this work. There would be no need to read further. However, Adam and Eve, as all of us, were given the freedom to choose. They chose, and their choice had consequences, even as today there are consequences for the choices we make, including our choices when in conflict.

Discerning "Scripts"

Ancient families, as families today, exhibit both commonalities and differences in their approach to conflict. Not all are alike. Family conflict DNAs do exist, even within singular cultures. These have sometimes been referred to as "scripts." In some families, as one example, words fly easily in the face of conflict, while in other families members retreat into silence. The variations are many.

A modern story that well illustrates a script is told by David Brinkley, the veteran twentieth-century, American newscaster. In his book on the transformation of Washington D.C. during World War II, he tells of a Washington 1940s nightclub frequented by members of the different branches of the U.S. military. Rivalry among these branches frequently led to conflict and even outbreaks of fighting. It happened so often that the management of the establishment posted a plan—a "script"—for dealing with the outbreaks, which was posted in the work area for the benefit of the employees. When conflicts escalated to fights, employees were instructed first to bring down the house lights in the dining area, second to turn on the spotlight focused on the large American flag which hung from the ceiling of the room, third to turn on a fan focused on the flag so it would flutter in the breeze, fourth to stop the dance music and have the band strike up the national anthem, and finally to call the military patrol and the navy's shore patrol in case they would yet be needed. If by the end of the national anthem, these symbols of national unity had not been sufficient to divert the attention of everyone from fighting to respectful attention, Brinkley reports, the military police and navy shore patrol would be coming up the steps ready to quell the disturbance. Then Brinkley adds: "It always worked."[4] That is a script—a patterned response to conflict. Whether consciously written or not, we all have scripts—as did the ancient families of Genesis, as we will discover. The good news is that while our families of origin shape us, they need not determine forever what we do. We are free to test our inheritance, and if need be, to choose better ways.

In brief, then, motivation for this work springs from my belief in human freedom, in the significance of beginnings as points of moral reference and clarity from which we can learn, and in the need to choose wisely as we construct scripts as pathways that lead to where peace is at home in our time.

PART I
Genesis: Beginning Pathways

Take your Bible and take your newspaper, and read both.
But interpret newspapers from your Bible.
– Karl Barth, *Time*, May 31, 1963

When I was a child, I read these Biblical tales
with a wonder mixed with anguish.
I imagined Isaac on the altar and I cried.
I saw Joseph, prince of Egypt, and I laughed...

...All the legends, all the stories retold by the Bible...involve us.
That of the first killer as well as that of the first victim.
We have but to reread them to realize that they are surprisingly topical.
Job is our contemporary.
-Elie Wiesel, *Messengers of God: Biblical Portraits and Legends*

God made man because he loves stories.
-Elie Wiesel

CHAPTER 1
Murder: Cain and Abel

Genesis 4 - 9

ANCIENT HEADLINES
(as they might have appeared in today's media)

Brother Kills Brother in Field

Husband Imitates Cain in Killing of Adversary

Epidemic of Violence Explodes in the World

Flood Forecast as Response to Violence

TODAY'S HEADLINES
(as they have appeared in today's media)

Youth held over brother's murder
Arab News (Jeddah, Saudi Arabia), August 16, 2010

Man on trial in brother's murder takes the stand
Virgin Islands Daily News, February 17, 2005

Man Kills Wife Over Affair
The Times of India, December 19, 2010

Ex-Couple's Quarrel Ends in Killing and Suicide
The New York Times, November 4, 2006

My wife and I, along with our three school-age children, wound our way through the pre-dawn streets of East Jerusalem to the Mount of Olives on Easter Sunday morning of April 11, 1982. We were on our way to the sunrise service of Jerusalem's Lutheran Church of the Redeemer. Facing east on the ridge of the Mount, we worshipped with fellow early risers and waited for the sun to appear over the hazy Jordan River valley below.

As we descended the western slope of the Mount on our return, we paused in an old olive orchard overlooking the old city for a breakfast of oranges and traditional Easter bread with colored eggs, which we had purchased the previous day. As we ate, a lone rider on a donkey appeared in the valley below slowly finding his way along the eastern wall of the old city. It was as though nothing had changed over the centuries.

Rising majestically across the valley was the golden Dome of the Rock, situated on what Muslims call the Noble Sanctuary and Jews the Temple Mount. In no other place on earth do the Abrahamic religions come together with the intensity that they do here. Each has their designated place for worship. The Mount itself is reserved for Muslim worship with its holy sites of the Dome of the Rock and the Al-Aqsa Mosque. The adjacent Wailing Wall is reserved for Jews. For Christians, either constitutes a place of pilgrimage.

As we returned to our place of residence, we walked through the Muslim section of the old city entering by St. Stephen's gate on the east wall and exiting by the north Damascus Gate. About the same time, Alan Harry Goodman, an American Jewish transplant from Baltimore, was finding his way through another part of the old city. He wore an Israeli army uniform and carried an M-16 automatic rifle. He shot his way into the Noble Sanctuary, killing one Muslim and wounding at least four others, while simultaneously spraying the Dome of the Rock with bullets, before he was apprehended.

Goodman chose the pathway earlier forged by Cain; namely, to eliminate the other with whom one is in conflict. It is the first post-Eden pathway portrayed in the book of Genesis. Immediately after the narrative of Adam and Eve's banishment from the idyllic Garden of Eden, we are thrust into a story of murder.

Erik Barnouw, in *Tube of Plenty*, his classic study of the history of American television, notes that in the early years of television programming one instruction given to television script writers was as follows: "It has been found that we retain audience interest best when our story is concerned with murder. Therefore, although other crimes may be introduced, somebody must be murdered, preferably early, with the threat of more violence to come."[1]

We may wonder whether our Genesis storyteller of long ago was likewise advised. But the first post-Eden story of Cain's murder of his brother has to do with more than capturing audience interest. For the story has to do with that primal urge to eliminate the other who is blocking our way when in conflict. That urge has persisted from Cain to the present. So this primal urge is well placed at the beginning of the post-Eden portion of Genesis as our first pathway for dealing with conflict. It is the first reality we must confront.

The Story

Unlike the later Genesis family stories of the three great patriarchs—Abraham, Isaac and Jacob—this first post-Eden story is not complicated by relationships between parents and children. Father Adam and Mother Eve do not appear in this story beyond a brief beginning report of the births of their two sons, Cain and Abel. They then disappear from the narrative. Remaining is a triangle of characters; namely, the two brothers and God, who functions in the story as the eternal parent.

We are told that the first son, Cain, was a farmer, "a tiller of the ground." Abel, his younger brother, was a shepherd. Both were religious and dutifully brought sacrifices of what they produced to God. Cain's offering is simply noted as being "the fruit of the ground;" Abel's is further qualified as being "the firstlings of his flock, their fat portions." Whether for this reason or another, God accepted Abel's offering, but not Cain's.

In response to God's rejection of his apparent ordinary offering, we are told that "Cain was very incensed, and his face fell"[2] Or, as interpreted in ancient rabbinic literature, "His face turned as red as a torch"[3] Our faces bear first witness when our honor is compromised. Cain's face fell.

Seeing Cain's anger and fallen face, God counseled him: "Why are you angry, and why has your countenance [face] fallen? If you do well, will you not be accepted? [or your face be up-lifted?] And if you do not do well, sin is lurking at the door; its desire is for you, but you must master it."

Loss of face is a powerful driver of violence. After working for a quarter century with persons incarcerated for the most violent crimes, psychiatrist James Gilligan observes: "I have yet to see a serious act of violence that was not provoked by the experience of feeling shamed and humiliated, disrespected and ridiculed, and that did not represent the attempt to prevent or undo this 'loss of face'—no matter how severe the punishment, even if it includes death."[4]

How, then, might face be restored without resorting to violence? Australian criminologist John Braithwaite helpfully distinguishes between "reintegrative shaming" and "disintegrative shaming." The latter results from "stigmatization" as in attaching a negative label to a wrongdoer (e.g. criminal, juvenile delinquent, and the like). "Reintegrative shaming," in contrast, "means that expressions of community disapproval…are followed by gestures of reacceptance into the community…"[5] In our story God respectfully confronted Cain, and did not add to his shame by labeling or stigmatizing him as an unacceptable outcast. Rather, God directed Cain to what it would take for him to reintegrate into community: "If you do well, will you not be accepted? [or your face be up-lifted]. And if you do not do well, sin is lurking at the door; its desire is for you, but you must master it."

Unwilling to manage his anger and "do well," Cain instead planned a murder. He invited Abel to a deserted field, and there Cain killed him. Not equal to taking on God, who after all was the one who had judged his offering as inadequate, he directed his anger against his brother, as students sometimes target the teacher's "pet" rather than the teacher.

Again God confronted Cain. "Where is your brother Abel?" God asked. "I do not know," Cain replied, "am I my brother's keeper?"

"Am I my brother's keeper?" We can thank Cain for asking the question, for it is the foundational moral question all of us as humans must address. The question lingers not only through the remaining Genesis narratives, as we shall see, but through all history to the present.

At the moment, nevertheless, God observed that Cain's denial of knowledge of the whereabouts of his brother was countered by the evidence: "Listen; your brother's blood is crying out to me from the ground!" Rabbi Aryeh Kaplan translates the Hebrew in *The Living Torah* even more forcefully: "The voice of your brother's blood is screaming to Me from the ground."

German commentator Klaus Westermann declares this statement to be "the high point of the narrative" and "one of the monumental sentences in the Bible." For if no one else hears the cry of one murdered, we can be assured that God does.[6]

But there is further significance in the statement. Contemporary commentators such as Westermann follow ancient rabbis of the Mishnah (ca 200 CE) and the subsequent Jerusalem and Babylonian Talmuds (commentaries) in noting that "blood" in the Hebrew text is in the plural. The Hebrew text actually reads: "…your brother's *bloods* are crying [screaming] out to me from the ground" (italics mine). The inference is that murder is always plural. Not only has the immediate Abel been killed, but also all the generations that would have come from him. Ancient rabbis then coined the phrase: "…whoever destroys a single soul is deemed [by Scripture] as if he had destroyed a whole world. And whoever saves a single soul is deemed by Scripture as if he had saved a whole world."[7]

This rabbinic interpretation of Cain's murder, furthermore, is also found in the Qur'an. Sura (chapter) 5:32 states: "On account of [Cain's deed], We decreed to the Children of Israel that if anyone kills a person—unless in retribution for murder or spreading corruption in the land—it is as if he kills all mankind, while if any saves a life it is as if he saves the lives of all mankind."[8]

Cain's guilt declared, God sentenced him to banishment: "... now you are cursed from the ground, which has opened its mouth to receive your brother's blood from your hand. When you till the ground, it will no longer yield to you its strength; you will be a fugitive and a wanderer on the earth."

Cain quickly appealed: "My punishment is greater than I can bear! Today you have driven me away from the soil, and I shall be hidden from your face; I shall be a fugitive and a wanderer on the earth, and anyone who meets me may kill me."

"Not so!", God responded. "Whoever kills Cain will suffer a sevenfold vengeance." God then placed on Cain a special mark that assured the preservation of his life. This mark, not described, apparently did not stigmatize him as a murderer; rather, it was a mark that somehow assured the preservation of his life.

Justice, in this first case of murder, was not served by a death sentence. On the contrary, Cain was assured that his life would be preserved, though under the harsh circumstances of a two-fold banishment; first from the ground, his familiar source of livelihood, and then from the face of God, the source of all life.

The Divine guarantee of life, furthermore, was assured by the threat of Divine vengeance against anyone who would take his life; indeed, "sevenfold vengeance", drawing on the Hebrew expression that was used to make a point most emphatically.

The Escalation of Violence

Like a contagious disease, Cain's murder soon spread to the neighborhood. One named Lamech, we are told, quickly followed in

Cain's steps. Lamech returned home one day and reported to his two wives, Adah and Zillah:

> I have killed a man for wounding me,
> a young man for striking me.
> If Cain is avenged sevenfold,
> truly Lamech seventy-sevenfold.

The formula for Lamech's vengeance was "seventy-sevenfold", thus even more emphatic than the "sevenfold" vengeance earlier promised by God against one who would kill Cain. God's vengeance, furthermore, was now preempted by Lamech. No waiting for God here. Lamech will take vengeance into his own hands.

The violence begun by Cain and escalated by Lamech continued to infect the ancient world until it became a major epidemic. God finally had enough, for as we are told, "...the earth was corrupt in God's sight, and the earth was filled with violence." Overwhelmed with the enormity of the violence, God said: "I will blot out from the earth the human beings I have created—people together with animals and creeping things and birds of the air, for I am sorry that I have made them."

Seven times in the first chapter of Genesis, as I earlier noted, God looked at what he had created and proclaimed it to be good. Indeed, the seventh time as "very good." Now, in the space of a few chapters, we are told that God was sorry that he had made them.

So God came to Noah and said: "I have determined to make an end of all flesh, for the earth is filled with violence because of them; now I am going to destroy them along with the earth." Having enough of violence, God brought on a great flood to destroy what had earlier been judged to be a masterpiece, saving only a remnant, including Noah and his family, to begin anew.

The story of this first post-Eden epidemic of violence thus ends with a new beginning. After the flood waters had subsided and the residents of the ark were back on dry land, God instructed Noah, as earlier he had instructed Adam, to "be fruitful and multiply, and fill the earth." God then added a new principle of justice designed to curb the unrestrained violence of the pre-flood era: "Whoever sheds the blood of a human, by a human shall that person's blood be shed." God further grounded this principle in the moral precept: "for in his own image God made humankind."

But what about God's own violence of the great flood? God followed by adding a personal commitment never again to repeat the violence of the great flood itself: "…never again shall all flesh be cut off by the waters of a flood, and never again shall there be a flood to destroy the earth." God placed a rainbow in the sky as symbol of his commitment.

Noah, on the other hand, was not in a position similarly to bind his descendants to abstain from pursuing the pathway of violence. A double rainbow did not appear in the sky. So while we as humans live under the rainbow of God, violence continues to be part of our human experience. We may then well ask, how are we who live in this twenty-first century of the common era doing?

Cain Our Contemporary

Violence, sadly, did not drown in the great flood. The world's media daily bear witness. James, who was in a difficult divorce process, gunned down his wife and her attorney, killing them both, after which he fatally shot himself. Khan, suspecting his wife was having an extramarital affair, beat her with a stick, after which she died. Scott, who opposed doctors whose practice included abortions, shot and killed Dr. George while he was handing out bulletins as usher in his church one Sunday morning. Fourteen-year-old Brandon shot and killed Lawrence, his fellow junior high school student, who had let the students of his school know that he was gay. High school coach Ed was shot and killed by Mark, who once played for him at the school. An unnamed Florida high schooler stabbed and killed his fellow student Juan, apparently in a dispute over a girl. Nathaniel, who was fired from his position as a custodian, shot and killed Larry, a building services manager.

If I would account in the same manner for each murder in our world during the first decade-and-a-half of this twenty-first century, I would need to add about six million sentences. That is the estimated number of murders that the World Health Organization (WHO) reports occurred between its first 2002 *World Report on Violence and Health*, with statistics based on the year 2000, and its follow-up *Global Status Report on Violence Prevention 2014*, "making homicide a more frequent cause of death than all wars combined during this period." Since 2014, daily homicides have continued while also punctuated by periodic mass shootings in schools, workplaces, entertainment venues, and the like. God, indeed, has had an earful of cries of the blood of those murdered.

Murder, however, is only one of three categories of violent deaths in WHO's profile of our world. In its first 2002 report based on the first year of this century, an estimated 1.6 million died in just that one year with self-inflicted violence as in suicide constituting about half (49.1%), interpersonal violence as in murder about a third (31.3%), and war-related deaths almost a fifth (18.6%).[9]

As with Cain, relationships gone awry have led to most violent deaths, whether with oneself, others, or collectivities of various sorts. So it was in twentieth-century America where "about three out of four homicides" throughout the century involved killers and victims who were acquainted.[10] Add to that the more than 100 million who died in last century's wars as a result of relationships gone awry between and among nations. Murder did "not really come into its own" until last century, in the view of Colin Wilson, English philosopher and writer on crime.[11] But war, too, could be viewed as not really having come into its own until last century with war deaths exceeding all previous centuries. As the violence of Cain escalated to where the earth was filled with violence, so it has also been in our time.

Whereas relationships gone awry have led to most violence, killings by strangers do happen. The daily news reports tend to feature such killings. Witness the media attention given in the United States to the 1993 kidnapping by a stranger of twelve-year-old Polly Klaas in Petaluma, California, my home state. Anxious day followed anxious day of search, all well reported in the media, only in the end leading to the discovery of her lifeless body.

A stranger breaking into a home, kidnapping and then killing a child is a horrible thing. Yet Kenneth Lanning, special supervisory agent at the FBI Academy's Behavioral Science Unit in Quantico, Virginia, poignantly observed at the time: "In the two months that you put all this energy and these resources into one child who's been abducted, 200 kids [in the United States alone] are murdered by their mother or father."[12]

Recent moments of hope, moreover, have soon given way to despair. Late last century, the end of the "Cold War" was one such moment. But the hopeful declaration of a "new world order" quickly gave way to redirected human animosities as "across the old empire," Strobe Talbott of *Time* magazine observed at the time, "neighbors turned enemies are invoking their right of self-determination as they slit one another's throats."[13] In Africa, Cain's fury was matched by Rwandan Hutus, who in the space of 100 days, with weapons hardly advanced beyond those available to Cain, managed to kill some 800,000 of their fellow Tutsi. In a more protracted, internal war beginning in the mid-1990s, more than five million are estimated to have died in the Democratic Republic of Congo.

The World Council of Churches' hopeful *Decade to Overcome Violence* beginning our twenty-first century is more needed than ever. My own country is exhibit one. For in America, proclaimed in song to be "the beautiful," the "risk of being murdered is higher than it is in any other first-world democracy," as reported by Randolph Roth in his extensive 2009 study of *American Homicide*. Neighboring Canada, "the next most homicidal affluent democracy," as Roth reports, "has had only a quarter of the homicides per capita that the United States has had since World War II."[14] Future prospects are not hopeful. Given an American life expectancy of seventy-eight years and continuing murders at the average rate of the past, Roth projects that Americans can expect that one of every 142 children born today will be murdered—1 of every 460 white girls, 1 of every 158 white boys, 1 of every 112 nonwhite girls, and 1 of every 27 nonwhite boys.[15] Given the disproportionate prospects for people of color, one can understand why the slogan, "Black Lives Matter," is so compelling.

"Guns don't kill, people kill," is a common mantra of our time. Yet when consumed by anger, people grab whatever instrument of killing is within reach, whether a stick, stone, knife or gun. The reality is that since Cain, more and more devastating means of killing have come into the reach of more and more angry people. The wrestling arm and boxing fist, earlier extended by the knife, sword and spear, in modern times have been further extended by the gun and assorted varieties of bombs, and ultimately the atomic bomb. The reach of the eye has been multiplied through radar and satellite systems. And where once one would reach one's opponent by foot and wheel, today not only do airplanes and rockets deliver their devastating warheads and bombs, but unmanned drones wind their way to distant and unsuspecting targets. On occasion these delivery systems themselves are turned into weapons as on September 11, 2001, the airplane became a fist-bomb aimed at the heart of the financial–military complex of the United States.

To all of this, God says "no." God's "no" to Cain, furthermore, is confirmed by the Mosaic commandment prohibiting murder (Exodus 20:13) and the New Testament's emphatic declaration: "We must not be like Cain…" (1 John 3:12).

The Celebration of Life

A "no," nevertheless, also implies a "yes." God's "yes" is to life, given that we are all created in the image of God. That, too, we learn from this first post-Eden story of Genesis.

So though the pathway of Cain is still very much with us, on occasion the ancient rabbinic interpretation of the Cain and Abel story affirming life is also resurrected in surprising ways. It was so in October of 1939 when Itzhak Stern, a Jewish survivor of the Holocaust, quoted the rabbinic interpretation of the story—"He who saves the life of one man saves the entire world"—to German industrialist Oskar Schindler. Novelist Thomas Keneally notes: "Itzhak, rightly or wrongly, always believed that it was at that moment that he had dropped the right seed in the furrow."[16] Schindler subsequently saved the lives of many Jews by insisting to Nazi authorities that he needed them as employees in the making of products vital to the war effort.

In 1945, before parting after the war had ended, the surviving Jews of Schindler's factory presented him with a gift. The gift was a ring fashioned by a former jeweler among them named Licht. For material, he used the gold bridgework taken from the mouth of another surviving worker in the factory. He then inscribed on its inner circle, in Hebrew, the saying: "He who saves a single life saves the world entire."[17] This saying now appears on the sign fronting Schindler's factory-turned-museum, which opened in Kraków, Poland in 2010.

But the saying is more than a museum piece remembering the past. It continues to resonate with those who struggle against violence. So in this violent second decade of this twenty-first century, the saying reappeared on the cover of *Time* magazine (October 17, 2016), now taken from the Qur'an's parallel interpretation of the Cain and Abel story. *Time's* cover story featured the "White Helmets" rescuers of persons injured by the horrific fighting in Syria. Their credo, appearing on *Time's* cover, is the Qur'an's rendition of the saying: "Whoever saves one life, saves all of humanity" (Sura 5:32). Sixty-thousand lives, *Time* reported, had already been saved by these courageous good Samaritans in the midst of the Syrian carnage.

This celebration of life is also captured well in the Hebrew toast, "*L'Chaim, L'Chaim*" ("to life, to life"). In similar fashion, John Donne (ca 1571-1631) long ago uttered those famous words: *No man [or person] is an island entire of itself.... Any man's [or person's] death diminishes me, because I am involved in Mankind.* So it is that the Genesis affirmation of life is not only for my people, but for all humankind. All are created in the image of God. While I intensely feel the death of a person close to me, the death of a foreigner also diminishes me because I am part of a greater humanity, as Donne reminds me.

Ambiguities

Ambiguities, nevertheless, remain. Though God placed a rainbow in the sky with the promise to never again bring on a great flood, how are we yet to understand the continuing violence of God as exhibited in the drowning of an Egyptian army in the Red Sea on the later occasion of Israel's liberating exit from Egypt, or the violence commanded by God in Israel's conquest of ancient Palestine, or the violence resulting from God's judgement of the nations as pronounced by the Hebrew prophets?

Likewise, how are we to understand the more immediate principle of equivalency represented by "blood for blood" as it evolved in the Mosaic law to an "eye for eye, tooth for tooth, hand for hand, foot for foot, burn for burn, wound for wound, stripe for stripe" (Exodus 21:23-25)? The same principle continues in modern justice. Today, mostly this "comes down to assigning various numbers of years [in prison] to different offenses depending on their badness," as William Ian Miller has observed, "years thus providing the means and measure of payment, rather than eyes, teeth, lives, or money."[18] Punishment must fit the crime, as we say today.

Violence, moreover, is inherent in this approach to justice, as psychiatrist James Gilligan has observed. "What is conventionally called 'crime' is the kind of violence that the legal system calls illegal, and 'punishment' is the kind that it calls legal."[19] Equivalent violence, as in "blood for blood," nevertheless, is intended to curb violence, as in the Genesis account it invalidates Cain's unequivalent murder in response to a rejected offering, along with Lamech's murder of one who had merely hit and wounded him. The basic principle is that one cannot take more than has been taken, or judgment cannot exceed the crime.

Equivalency, nevertheless, was not God's first word in response to murder, nor we may question whether it is his last. In the case of Cain, as earlier noted, God did not require equivalent "blood for blood," but placed that mysterious mark on him precisely to preserve his life. And if we look further through time, Jesus later challenged the principle of equivalency as expressed by "an eye for an eye and a tooth for a tooth" in his Sermon on the Mount. Hence, there is more to say about what constitutes justice, which I will explore further in Part II of this work.

While the Hebrew Bible leaves us with questions, the Qur'an, likewise, offers its own ambiguities in its interpretation of the Cain and Abel story. Sura 5:32's declaration, "Whoever saves one life, saves all of humanity," while surely positive, is not the full text. The full text reads in translation, as previously cited: "On account of [Cain's deed], We decreed to the Children of Israel that if anyone kills a person—unless in retribution for murder or spreading corruption in the land—it is as if he kills all mankind, while if any saves a life it is as if he saves the lives of all mankind."

Irshad Manji, a contemporary Muslim journalist, refers to the phrase—"unless in retribution for murder or spreading corruption in the land"—as an exception clause.[20] "Corruption in the land," in particular, opens the door to a wide range of interpretations. Those who kill to rid a land of those who do not share their faith, view of justice or political orientation, seeing them as corruption in the land, find justification for their murderous activities in such clauses. Others, such as the White Helmets saviors in the Syrian conflict earlier noted, find inspiration in "whoever saves one life, saves all of humanity," another clause of the text. Both peace-loving saviors and so-called terrorists find justification for their behaviors in the same text, though in different clauses.

Further ambiguities exist when violence escalates to war. As our Genesis account limits violence by invoking the principle of equivalency, so those who see war as a means of achieving justice on a larger scale have likewise established rules to limit the violence. Common among them is the prohibition against targeting civilians in warfare. Yet of the more than 100 million who died as a result of twentieth-century wars, the majority were civilians, notwithstanding this cardinal principle. After researching civilian deaths in wars conducted between 1816 and 2003, political scientist Alexander B. Downes concluded that "the norm against inflicting widespread and systematic harm on non-combatants in warfare is a frail one."[21] Democracies have not been exempt. Indeed, Downes's research led him to conclude that in protracted wars, democracies have been "more likely to target noncombatants than nondemocracies" as tiring populations pressure leaders "to end the war more quickly and save the lives of their own soldiers." As Downes observes, "while democracies may be slow to anger, once aroused by costly or protracted warfare, they fight with a fury."[22] Witness the earlier dropping of atomic bombs on the civilian populations of Hiroshima and Nagasaki in an effort to bring WWII to an end, along with the devastating fire bombing of civilians in enemy cities of both Europe and Japan. And consider the more recent breach of the prohibition against waterboarding and other varieties of torture in a desperate effort to elicit information from enemy prisoners of war. And that, too, perpetrated by an assumed, enlightened democracy.

So the struggle continues, whether Jew, Christian, Muslim or simply citizen. Sacred texts are read selectively and differently. What should be normative is debated. And being human, that primal impulse to eliminate the other blocking our way has a long history of overpowering professed norms to the contrary or counsel to manage one's anger and reintegrate into community, even if coming from our eternal parent God.

Yet that God said "no" to Cain's pathway of murder and the escalated violence of the ancient world is at least a beginning. Underlying this "no" is the foundational value that as humans we are all created in the image of God. And being so, we are called to discern alternative pathways as we seek to be our brother's and sister's keeper. So we turn next to how the patriarchal families of Abraham, Isaac and Jacob struggled toward alternatives as these may also inform alternative pathways for our time.

BEST PRACTICE

Our Genesis story of Cain and Abel is preceded by the story of creation. This first story is climaxed by God forming Adam and Eve, their parents, out of dust and a rib. Life for these two then began in a verdant garden called Eden, but was quickly marred when they yielded to the temptation of an evil serpent.

Likewise, the adult story of Rabbi Jesus in the second part of this work also began with a temptation. But whereas Eve and Adam yielded, Jesus did not.

The underlying truth of both stories is that a first step on the pathway to peace in the *shalom* truth and justice sense of the Hebrew Bible (Old Testament for Christians) is refusing to cooperate with evil in this world in all of its multiple forms including not only murder, but also lying, stealing, cheating, and all the endless forms of corruption and injustice. Murder, of course, is an extreme form of evil in this world. That was Cain's temptation. As told in this chapter, ancient rabbis saw two lessons in this story of these sons of Adam and Eve. Taking another's life is like taking the entire world – not only Abel in this case, but also all of those who would have descended from him. On the other hand, saving a life is also like saving the entire world, including all the descendants of the one whose life is saved.

So I suggest that as we begin our journey through the family stories of Genesis, we consider as "best practices" both a negative and a positive.

First, refuse to cooperate with evil in whatever form it may come, murder among them. For temptations will come, and choices will have to be made.

Second, as a guiding star, embrace the life-giving maxim suggested by ancient rabbis, repeated in the Qur'an, and embraced by saviors in our time: "Whoever saves one life saves the world entire." So as we walk the pathway to peace, pursue life rather than death.

With these in place, we can move on to explore alternative ways in which our very human Genesis families struggled in their own time to be their brothers' and sisters' life-giving keepers, both failing and succeeding. They model for us both positive and negative behaviors still relevant in our everyday lives.

CHAPTER 2
Separation: Abraham and Sarah

Genesis 11-25

ANCIENT HEADLINES
(as they might have appeared in today's media)

Uncle and Nephew Separate Over Limited Resources

Servant Runs Away from Abuse of Mistress

Second Wife and Son Expelled from Home

Well Diggers "Lump It"

TODAY'S HEADLINES
(as they have appeared in today's media)

Divorces rise as rules more flexible
China Daily, May 17, 2004

Expulsions Rise as Schools Get Tough on Violence
The Washington Post, July 10, 1994

Client conflicts led to breakup of merged firm
Indianapolis Business Journal, August 2, 2004

Israelis Build Wall To Separate From West Bank
Getty Images, December 3, 2002

"Divorce was always an option, not murder!", a mother screamed one day in court to her son-in-law who had been convicted of murdering his wife, her daughter. Who could argue with her? Even young Larry in *Children's Letters to God* understands that separating is better than killing. He writes: "Dear God, Maybe Cain and Abel would not kill each so much if they had their own rooms. It works with my brother."[1]

Abraham and Sarah, too, experienced separation in their lives. Indeed, their faith journey began with separation in response to God's call to a new mission in a new land. Our Genesis narrator reports:

> Now the Lord said to Abram, "Go from your country and your kindred and your father's house to the land that I will show you. I will make of you a great nation, and I will bless you and make your name great, so that you will be a blessing. I will bless those who bless you, and the one who curses you I will curse; and in you all the families of the earth shall be blessed."

In this new beginning, God affirmed his desire that all of the families of the earth should be blessed. This universal blessing was now to come, however, through a special people who hopefully would model God's way in the world. Disobedience and violence had been the first human responses to God's great creative activity. Might this new strategy now produce something different?

One approach to change is to create a model that others may emulate. "Most human behavior is learned by observation through modeling," social scientist Albert Bandura has observed.[2] This is true of both individual, family and institutional behaviors. As humans we identify certain persons as model people, families as model families, and institutions as model institutions. God's intention for Abraham and Sarah was that they would parent a people who would model holiness as their Creator was holy, and so influence all of creation for good. Even model families and institutions, however, have their struggles. Abraham and Sarah were no exception. They continually danced between the larger vision of God and the everyday realities of living together. Our focus in this chapter is these everyday realities.

Negotiated Separation
Genesis 13-14, 18-19

Abraham's first home was Ur of the Chaldeans, located in what today we know as Iraq. In Ur Abraham had a brother named Haran, who had a son named Lot. Before Abraham left Ur to emigrate to the promised land, Haran died, leaving his son Lot. Abraham fulfilled his brotherly responsibility and took his nephew Lot under his wing. Sometime later in their new land, Uncle Abraham and nephew Lot, now an adult, developed a problem. Each had become so prosperous with "flocks and herds and tents" that the land could not support both of them. This problem of limited resources escalated into quarreling between their herdsmen. In response, Uncle Abraham took what inevitably must be a first step in peacemaking. He invited Lot to meet with him to address the problem.

When they met, Abraham began by setting forth the moral foundation for negotiation. He said to Lot: "Let's not have any quarreling between you and me, or between your herdsmen and mine, **for we are brothers**" (NIV – my bold). The older King James version—"for we be brethren"—has a wonderful ring to it. Brothers or brethren, however, is often translated as "kinsmen" in contemporary English versions of the Bible. "Kinsmen," however, obscures the connection of the text to the earlier question of Cain: "Am I my brother's keeper?" For the root Hebrew word for brother used by Abraham is the same as in Cain's earlier question. It is important not to miss this connection. For Abraham, not only should we not kill each other as brothers, but we also should not quarrel.

Current negotiation theory is deeply rooted in pragmatism—what works. Popular titles or subtitles of books entice their potential readers with phrases like "Negotiating Agreement Without Giving In," "How to…Get the Best Out of Bargaining," or generally how to win in negotiation. Abraham, however, began by setting forth the moral foundation for negotiation. Because we are brothers and sisters, we must not quarrel, but resolve our conflicts peaceably.

It is also important to note what Abraham is not saying. Abraham does not say it is wrong to have a problem. Having a problem in itself is no sin. Indeed, the problem here arises because of prosperity and wealth, which in Genesis are customarily attributed to God's blessing. But quarreling about the problem rather than finding a constructive solution is the antithesis of being a brother or sister. So Abraham posits his premise: we are brothers, so we must not quarrel.

Having established the premise for negotiation, Abraham proceeded by proposing the solution of separation, but then gave Lot, though the younger, the first choice as to which direction he would go: "If you take the left hand, then I will go to the right; or if you take the right hand, then I will go to the left." His approach is akin to a person cutting the last piece of pie, and then giving the other first choice lest she be accused of unfairly dividing the piece and then taking the best. In our story, Lot proceeded to choose the best—the lush Jordan River valley over the rocky hill country—and Abraham honored his choice.

Hebrew scholar Robert Alter, in a footnote in his translation of Genesis, notes that in this negotiation "the language in which Abraham addresses Lot is clear, firm, and polite."[3] I would add, generous. A wonderful formula for negotiation. Uncle Abraham had mastered the art of constructive negotiation, and nephew Lot was cooperative and agreeable. They separated peacefully.

Separation, though, is not the end of the story. Separation did not end the relationship. Abraham continued to be a brother to Lot. When neighboring kings conquered the valley kings where Lot had moved, including his hometown of Sodom, and took Lot and his family captive along with the rest, it was Abraham who went to his rescue. Later, when some visitors arrived at his tent flap, including "the Lord," and informed him that Sodom would be destroyed because of its wickedness, it was again Abraham who intervened on Lot's behalf. Drawing on his negotiation skills, he dared to challenge the Lord. If there are fifty righteous in Sodom, Abraham asked the Lord, will you really destroy it? And the Lord said no. What about forty-five? Again the Lord said no. What about forty? Thirty? Twenty? Finally, what if there are only "ten?" The Lord said he would preserve the entire city even if there were only ten righteous. But alas, there weren't even ten. Yet, in the end, the Lord did spare Lot and his family by pulling them out of Sodom before he rained down fire from heaven on the city and destroyed it.

In brief, then, Abraham had learned the answer to Cain's question: "Am I my brother's keeper?" Better to invite the other into negotiation over a problem than to quarrel. If separation then seems wise, the relationship, though changed, best remains positive and caring. Even through separation and the questionable choices of nephew Lot, Abraham modeled what it means to be a brother's keeper.

Running Away Separation
Genesis 16

When Abraham embarked on the last leg of his journey to the promised land from a place called Haran, he was seventy-five years old. Sarah was sixty-five. They were childless, though God had promised Abraham a son; indeed, "a great nation."

A famine in their new land caused Abraham and Sarah to travel for a time to Egypt, where the annual cycle of the Nile River provided a continuing source of food. It was likely on this journey that they acquired an Egyptian maid for Sarah named Hagar, who is a central figure in this story of running away.

Back in the promised land, some ten years after first arriving, Sarah, childless and seeing no hope of becoming pregnant, suggested to Abraham that he take her Egyptian servant girl Hagar as a second wife, and through her have a child that Sarah could call her own, according to the custom of the time. They would then have a child to inherit their estate. Abraham, who was eighty-five years old at the time, accepted the counsel of his seventy-five-year-old wife, and young Hagar became pregnant by Abraham.

Sarah's desperate alternative to barrenness, however, led to an unfortunate consequence. For Hagar, now pregnant, developed an attitude of superiority to Sarah. Indeed, our Genesis storyteller says, "she looked with contempt on her mistress." In cultures where child bearing is inextricably linked with a woman's identity, women who are barren sometimes suffer at the hands of others, even today. So Hagar's attitude of superiority is understandable, even if not excusable.

Sarah, unhappy with this turn of events, complained to her husband. Abraham, in turn, gave her the freedom to deal with the situation as she wished, though we may be surprised with his seemingly cavalier response given that Hagar was carrying the child that was to be the solution to their problem of inheritance. Yet, his behavior was consistent with the provisions of the Sumerian legal culture of his native Ur, which permitted upstart secondary wives to be put back in their place as servants.[4] Sarah, accordingly, treated Hagar harshly.

Hagar, nevertheless, too had limits. She experienced that proverbial "straw that broke the camel's back," and ran away. On her way, however, Hagar was found by the "angel of the Lord" by a spring in the wilderness. The angel inquired: "Hagar, slave-girl of Sarai, where have you come from and where are you going?" Her response indicates no destination. Rather, she truthfully reported: "I am running away from my mistress Sarai." Her focus was on getting away. Where she was going was secondary, which is not uncommon among runaways in conflictual and abusive relationships.

The angel's response was to send her back. "Return to your mistress, and submit to her," the angel said. Then the angel added a promise: "I will so greatly multiply your offspring that they cannot be counted for multitude." The angel further took note of her pregnancy, and informed her that she would bear a son who was to be named Ishmael, meaning "the Lord has given heed to your affliction" [i.e. "ill-treatment" or "harassment"]; that is, the Lord has heard you.

As Abel's screaming blood had earlier reached the ears of God, so now Hagar's "affliction," too, was heard by God. Ishmael, the name to be given to Hagar's child, was a constant reminder that God had heard.

While the angel took note of her situation, the angel nevertheless sent her back, even though there was no promise or expectation that the harsh treatment of Sarah would cease. Indeed, as noted above, Hagar was counseled by the angel not only to return, but also to "submit" to her mistress.

Hagar obediently returned, and gave birth to a son. Father Abraham named him Ishmael, as instructed by the angel. Abraham was eighty-six years old when Ishmael was born; Sarah was seventy-six. We are not given Hagar's age.

Hagar, of course, is not alone in choosing to run away from conflict in this world. Throughout history, children and adults alike have followed her lead. The thought entered the mind of one of our daughters very early. While still a preschooler, now years ago, she appeared one evening at our kitchen table with her tiny tea set wondering whether we, her parents, would drive her out to the highway. She was ready to run away.

Even Charlie Brown, in the old Peanuts comic strip, decided one day to run away, with his knapsack slung over his shoulder. Snoopy, his dog, while keeping his distance, nevertheless trailed him wearing an official-looking hat and carrying a briefcase. Charlie's unsuccessful efforts to dissuade Snoopy from following him led to a final confrontation in which Snoopy blurted out in self defense: "I thought you might need an attorney."

In the United States the National Runaway Safeline reports that between 1.6 and 2.8 million American youth actually do run away in any single year. "One in five youth run away before reaching age eighteen, and half run away two or more times," according to a study of the Urban Institute. Causes are many including abuse, as in the case of Hagar, but also divorce, remarriage, problems with siblings, and the like. "High-conflict home environments" are a major contributing factor, as noted in "Why They Run," a 2010 study of "America's runaway youth."

While global statistics are difficult to discern, The United Nations Children's Fund (UNICEF) has estimated that as many as 100 million children in any year live on the streets of the world's cities, though "the exact number...is impossible to quantify." Not all, of course, are runaways. Some also have lost parents, been thrown out of families, or simply pushed out because of poverty.

Adults, too, are known to run from conflict. In John Updike's novel, *Rabbit, Run*, the main character, Rabbit Angstrom, is asked: "What's happened to your home?" He replies: "Well, it kind of went." When further asked: "How do you mean?", he replies: "It was no good. I've run out. I really have."[5]

Parents, too, may run away. A Valentine's day card once given by a daughter to my wife and me portrays a husband and wife in running attire, with the inscription below: "Mom and Dad, I'm sure you've thought of it a few times"—and then the inscription inside as one opens the card: "but thanks for not running away! Happy Valentine's Day."

And, of course, one can run away psychologically while physically staying at home by simply shutting down and refusing to communicate. The options are many.

Forced Separation
Genesis 21

Forced separation, too, comes in many forms. One may be thrown out of a home, pushed out of a marriage, expelled from school, fired from a position, dismissed from a leadership position, and the like.

Forced separation, too, was part of the experience of Abraham's family. The family experienced it both as victim and offender.

The experience of separation as victim occurs early in the Abraham narratives. The story begins with a journey from the promised land to Egypt in search of food due to a famine. Fearing that the Egyptians might kill him in order to secure his attractive wife, Abraham and Sarah identified each other as brother and sister rather than husband and wife. As expected, the Egyptians were drawn to Sarah's beauty. The princes of the country praised her to Pharaoh, the ruler of the land, and he took her into his harem. But Sarah was not good news for Pharaoh. Our storyteller tells us that "the Lord afflicted Pharaoh and his house with great plagues because of Sarai." When their deception was uncovered, Pharaoh confronted Abraham, gave Sarah back to him, and ordered them to "be gone." Pharaoh's men, we are told, set them on their way. Expelled from Egypt, they returned to the promised land.

A repeat of this experience occurred later in the promised land when in the territory of a local king named Abimelech. Again Abraham and Sarah played the roles of brother and sister out of fear that King Abimelech might kill Abraham to possess his wife. Again the deception was uncovered. But in this second experience the outcome was different. Abimelech, a seemingly wise king, and Abraham made peace with each other, and Abraham was permitted to remain in the region.

These stories reflect efforts to survive in the face of perceived threats from outsiders. But the key story of forced separation in the Abraham narrative grows out of the internal dynamics of the family itself.

When Abraham was eighty-six years old, as I have noted, Hagar gave birth to Ishmael. Some thirteen years later, Sarah miraculously became pregnant. She was eighty-nine. When full term at the age of ninety, Sarah gave birth to a son, who was named Isaac. Abraham was one-hundred. And Ishmael, now fourteen years old, was blessed with a half brother.

For Sarah, however, Ishmael now was no longer a blessed son she would call her own, as was her original plan. So one day when she saw

Ishmael playing with Isaac, she was not pleased. She demanded of Abraham: "Cast out this slave woman with her son; for the son of this slave woman shall not inherit along with my son Isaac."

Inheritance, as previously noted, was a key concern for both Abraham and Sarah. Already years ago, Abraham had complained to God: "You have given me no offspring, and so a slave born in my house is to be my heir." In this multi-ethnic family, this slave is identified as "Eliezer of Damascus," located in what is now Syria.

In response, God had assured Abraham that "no one but your very own issue shall be your heir." But years followed, as we know, and no heir was forthcoming. Sarah, as we are simply told, "bore him no children." Sarah, then, had said to Abraham, "go in to my slave-girl; it may be that I shall obtain children by her." And so it was.

Now, however, having her own son, Sarah's original idea of resolving the problem of inheritance was transformed into a new problem of shared inheritance, with the greater portion to the firstborn. Her resolution at this point was to draw the definition of family tightly. For her, Ishmael was no longer family.

Sarah's redefinition of family is reflected in her language. In her demand to Abraham to drive Hagar and Ishmael out, Sarah identified them not by name, but as "this slave woman with her son!" Am I then not my brother's or sister's keeper? Well, not if I can redefine persons in such a way that they are outside of the family, as later protagonists in history have defined groups of people and enemies as less than human. Once so defined, the ethics of being a brother's or sister's keeper simply no longer apply.

Abraham, however, was intensely disturbed by Sarah's demand. Though Sumerian law of his native Ur allowed contrary second wives to be put back into their place, it also provided certain protections for the Hagars and Ishmaels of the world. What Sarah was proposing ran contrary to that law.[6] Our Genesis storyteller informs us, nevertheless, that God counseled Abraham to proceed as Sarah had requested, but not without the significant promise that a nation would also come from Ishmael. So Abraham provided Hagar and Ishmael with some beginning provisions for their journey, and sent them off.

But what about a continuing relationship? I noted that in the case of Abraham's separation from Lot, the separation did not end the relationship. Abraham continued to care for Lot as his brother. So when Lot was taken captive together with the kings of the Jordan River valley, Abraham went to the rescue. And when word came that God was going to destroy the wicked cities of Sodom and Gomorrah, Abraham negotiated on behalf of Lot.

In the case of Abraham's forced separation from Hagar and Ishmael, however, the expulsion from the family seems to have ended the relationship. Our Genesis storyteller, however, does not forsake Hagar and Ishmael, but follows them on their journey into the wilderness, where they soon ran out of water. Desperate, facing death, an angel of God took the place of Abraham, and became their "keeper." The angel supplied them with water. In a concluding statement, moreover, our storyteller tells us that "God was with the boy, and he grew up; he lived in the wilderness, and became an expert with the bow."

Whereas Sarah rejected Hagar and Ishmael as family, for God they remained family. This truth has profound significance for contemporary Middle East politics, which is often driven by the "either-or" thinking of Sarah rather than the "both-and" thinking of God. So must one choose between those who find their identity in Isaac (Jews) and those who find their identity in Ishmael (Arabs, including Palestinians), both sons of Abraham?

In this story God, the eternal Parent, assigns different roles to these two sons of the Middle East. "...It is through Isaac that offspring shall be named for you," God said to Abraham. Simultaneously, a "great nation" was also to come from Ishmael. For God, as portrayed in this narrative, the selection of one son for a particular role did not necessitate the rejection of the other for another role. Both received promises from God. And God, we are told, was with both.

God's curses as well as his blessings were possibilities in this story. As earlier noted, when God called Abraham to leave his homeland and father a special people, God had said to him: "I will bless those who bless you, and the one who curses you I will curse." Moreover, God quickly followed this with a larger statement of purpose: "and in you all the families of the earth shall be blessed."

As a matter of logic, it makes little sense for God to curse a portion of his creation at the outset of a new strategy that promises that through Abraham "all the families of the earth shall be blessed." Indeed, the precondition for cursing—"the one who curses you I will curse"—is nowhere present in this story.

Rather, as those of low power in the structure of this ancient family, Hagar and Ishmael were victims of a struggle over the issue of inheritance—a struggle in which this ancient family first lamented the possibility of a slave, Eliezer of Damascus, inheriting the estate. Sarah's creative idea of having a child by her servant girl provided an alternative, which led to Ishmael displacing Eliezer. Ishmael, in turn, was displaced by Isaac. Yet, for God, Hagar and Ishmael remained family, which we can assume was also the case with Eliezer.

God's care for Hagar and Ishmael in the desert has been a source of comfort for contemporary Middle Eastern spiritual descendants of these two; among them, the father of Elias Chacour, a Palestinian Christian who lives in Israel. Chacour reports in *Blood Brothers* that in 1949 his father and older brothers were evicted from their Palestinian village by Israeli forces. They were trucked to a place distant from their village, and told to leave. Subjected to terror, the intent was to drive them from their homeland. For three months, however, they wandered through the countryside under the cover of night determined to find their way home. They finally arrived back in their home village in the dead of night, knocking on the door of their home where the women and younger children continued to live. Then Elias's father prayed the following prayer:

Father, they are treating us badly because we are the children of Ishmael. But we are true sons of Abraham—and your children. You saved Ishmael from death in the wilderness, and you have saved us. You brought justice for him and blessed him with a great nation. We thank you now, for we know that you will bring justice for us....[7]

For Elias, these and other words of his father have been a force for good in a context often driven by "either-or" rather than "both-and" thinking. So, when Elias's older brother, Rudah, brought a gun home to protect the family, Elias reports that his father lectured Rudah with words that appear in Chacour's book in italics for emphasis: "*The Jews and Palestinians are blood brothers. We must never forget that.*"[8]

The embrace of each other as blood brothers has led to at least some peace in the Middle East. For former King Hussein bin Talal of Jordan, this vision of blood brothers expressed in the phrase, "children of Abraham," was increasingly compelling in his later years, as noted by historian Nigel Ashton in his biography of the King.[9] "Perhaps his finest moment," as the king's Queen Noor describes it, occurred at the signing of the peace treaty between Jordan and Israel in 1994. In his address at the time, King Hussein observed: "For many, many years, and with every prayer, I have asked God, the Almighty, to help me be a part of forging peace between the children of Abraham. This was the dream of generations before me, and now I see it realized."[10]

A strong test of the depth of King Hussein's understanding of Jew and Arab as both children of Abraham occurred when seven Israeli schoolgirls were shot and killed and another six wounded on March 13, 1997, by a "deranged" Jordanian soldier while the children were on a school outing on the Island of Peace at a crossing of the Jordan River. Distressed by what a member of his army had done, "three days later Hussein made an unprecedented visit to the Israeli village of Beit Shemesh to offer his personal condolences to the families of the victims. At the homes of the stricken families, he went down on his knees and shared in their grief," though this expression of submission was offensive to others in the Arab world. Then, without publicity, he sent a million dollars to the bereaved families through President Ezer Weizman of Israel.[11]

Sadly, in our time many continue to be shaped in their approach to the Middle East by the exclusionary politics of Sarah. But God, as a principal player in this ancient drama, chose differently, as I have noted. That should be instructive for all who choose to impose either-or, exclusionary thinking on the politics of the Middle East.

Sarah died at the age of 127, but Abraham lived to be 175, and then he died. Ironically, with mother Sarah not present to protest, having died some forty-eight years before, Isaac and Ishmael reunited and together buried their father in a final act of unity.

The option of responding to conflicts by forcing separations, of course, remains. Forced separations are common at all levels of human relationships. Fences and walls, both physical and psychological, are built to enforce separations—sometimes to keep people in, sometimes to keep people out, and sometimes simply to keep people separate so they won't kill each other. Who can forget the Berlin Wall? Earlier the Great Wall of China? And more recently, the formidable "security" fence built by Israel to separate Palestinians from Israelis. And the barrier built by the United States on its Mexican border to curb illegal immigration.

At the level of nations, conflict has not only produced millions of deaths, as noted in the first chapter, but also generations of refugees who have chosen to flee or been forced to leave their homes. In the year 2000 the United Nations High Commissioner for Refugees (UNHCR), on the occasion of the fiftieth anniversary of that organization, published a seminal work on *The State of the World's Refugees: Fifty Years of Humanitarian Action.* In the "Preface" to the work, then UN Secretary General Kofi Annan speaks of refugees as "the problem of forced displacement," or, to use the language of this chapter, "forced separation."

The UNHCR began, Kofi Annan notes, as "a small organization, with a three-year mandate to help resettle European refugees who were still homeless in the aftermath of the Second World War." But it was not soon to end. "Decade by decade," Sadako Ogata, UNHCR high commissioner in the year 2000, writes: "major upheavals of the past half century—a seemingly unending string of conflicts and crises… have resulted in the displacement of tens of millions of people." At the time of the 2000 report, the UNHCR alone was assisting some "22 million people in every corner of the world." And it continues. As Sadako Ogata wrote at the time: "With over a million people forced to flee their homes in Kosovo, East Timor and Chechnya in the last year of the 20th century alone, it is clear that the problem of forced displacement has not gone away, and is likely to remain a major concern of the international community in the 21st century," as indeed it has. It did not take long. The mass migrations from North Africa and the Middle East in the second decade of the century have matched the refugee crises of the World War II period, which originally motivated the establishment of the UNHCR.

In the forward to the UNHCR report, Sadako Ogata concludes: "History has shown that displacement is not only a consequence of conflicts; it can also cause conflict. Without human security, there can be no peace and stability."

From families to the nations of this world, forced separation remains a part of our human experience. It is a pathway available at all levels of relationships, as it was to Sarah and Abraham, and one we as humans frequently exercise, for better or worse.

"Lumping It," or Nonresistance
Genesis 26

"Lumping it" is a colloquial expression meaning not to resist or fight a bad situation, but to let it go and move on. Genuine "lumping it," or nonresistance as it may also be called, is not postponing or harboring an issue for a time with the intent of later, at a more advantageous moment, resurrecting it; rather, it is simply letting go – leaving the situation behind as one moves on.

In the Genesis narratives, this pathway is best illustrated through a story drawn from the next generation of Isaac, son of Abraham and Sarah, who within time too became prosperous and wealthy. As we have already seen in the first story of Abraham and Lot in this chapter, wealth and prosperity in rural cultures can stretch available resources of land and water, creating conflict. This is as true today as it was then. I live in the central valley of California, where contention over water is an ongoing activity. I can resonate, then, with ancient stories about water wells, as in the case of our concluding separation story.

Isaac's servants, our Genesis storyteller tells us, dug a well in the valley of Gerar, where Isaac had been welcomed by the local king, Abimelech. It was a well fed by spring water. Once dug, local herdsmen "quarreled with Isaac's herders," insisting that "the water is ours." Rather than resist, or even invite them to negotiate, Isaac "lumped it" and simply moved on, naming the well *Esek*, meaning in Hebrew, "contention."

Having moved on, his servants dug a second well, and again the locals quarreled over it. Again Isaac chose not to make an issue of it, and so again he moved on, naming the well *Sitnah*, meaning "strife" or "enmity."

A third well was then dug, and this time the locals did not quarrel over it. Isaac then named this well *Rehoboth*, meaning "wide spaces or room." "Now the Lord has made room for us," Isaac concluded, "and we shall be fruitful in the land." The story then ends without further comment.

Isaac, in this story, demonstrates mastery of the option of "lumping it," or moving on, without any signs of bitterness or planned vengeance. In the end he found the space he needed, and was grateful.

The way of "lumping it," of course, too remains a pathway for us today. Not every issue is worth making a fuss about. Sometimes we just need to move on.

Conclusion

Separating in response to conflict was a common script in the family of Abraham and Sarah, as it remains a common script today. One may negotiate separations, run away, force separations, or simply move on by "lumping it."

For better or worse, separations come in many varieties. No formula can suggest precisely what to do when. Resolutions, as reflected in the family of Abraham, derive often from complicated family and organizational dynamics. Wisdom is knowing what to do when.

Abraham's negotiated separation, nevertheless, represents an ideal. His moral premise of inviting the other into negotiation rather than quarreling, if we are indeed brothers and sisters, is surely to be affirmed. And his clear, firm, polite and generous approach to negotiation is surely a model to be emulated. Likewise, his continuing care for his brother Lot after separating is surely exemplary. Lot, too, is to be affirmed for accepting Abraham's invitation and cooperating in finding a constructive resolution. When all parties in conflict work cooperatively together, positive outcomes are more likely.

Also instructive is the modeling of God in these stories. As the eternal parent, God has a way of stepping in when earthly parents are absent. When no one else hears, God hears. So it was with Hagar and Ishmael in the desert, as earlier with Abel's screaming blood. In the words of Quaker leader and scholar Douglas V. Steere, God is "the Eternal Listener." But in these early stories God does not stop with just listening. God also intervenes as the Eternal Counselor, Advocate and Judge.

Finally, there is the wisdom of Isaac, who determined that another option existed beyond fighting over a well, even if he had a rightful claim to it inasmuch as his servants had dug it. Rights notwithstanding, he moved on as in nonresistance, or "lumping it."

In brief, beyond murder there is the pathway of separation with all of its many possibilities. But we journey on as there are yet other pathways to explore.

BEST PRACTICE
Negotiation

Negotiation is an everyday experience in life. Spouses negotiate with each other over such simple things as where to go out to eat. Parents negotiate with their children, and children negotiate with their parents. Workers negotiate over wages and working conditions. Businesses negotiate over endless matters of concern. And so it goes, on and on. Abraham, in his negotiation with his nephew Lot, as told in this chapter, provides a model. As Hebrew scholar Robert Alter has noted in his translation of the biblical book of Genesis, Abraham's approach to negotiation can be characterized as "clear, firm, and polite."

In our time, Roger Fisher and William Ury of the Harvard Negotiation Project, in their path-breaking book, *Getting to Yes*, perhaps the most widely read book on negotiation in recent history, advocate a similar approach to negotiation. They advocate four basic principles:
1. Separate the People from the Problem
2. Focus on Interests, Not Positions
3. Invent Options for Mutual Gain
4. Insist on Objective Criteria

The first of these suggests treating the other with respect while engaging in mutual problem solving. Treat people as people separate from the problem. Abraham, many years ago, already modeled this principle. However, Roger Fisher and Scott Brown, both of the Harvard Negotiation Project, in *Getting Together: Building Relationships as We Negotiate,* provide additional specifics as to what this might entail. They suggest six principles under what they advocate as "an unconditionally constructive strategy." (Bold for emphasis is in the original)
1. **Rationality**. Even if they are acting emotionally, **balance emotions with reasons.**

2. **Understanding**. Even if they misunderstand us, **try to understand them.**
3. **Communication**. Even if they are not listening, **consult them before deciding** on matters that affect them.
4. **Reliability**. Even if they are trying to deceive us, neither trust them nor deceive them: **be reliable**.
5. **Noncoercive** modes of influence. Even if they are trying to coerce us, neither yield to that coercion nor try to coerce them: **be open to persuasion and try to persuade them.**
6. **Acceptance**. Even if they reject us and our concerns as unworthy of their consideration, **accept them as worthy of our consideration, care about them, and be open to learning from them.**

Abraham was not perfect. Today, wife Sarah and his treatment of Hagar would be questioned. But in his negotiation with his nephew over limited resources, he modeled "clear, firm and polite" negotiation that in our time has been elaborated by those associated with the Harvard Negotiation Project, as well as others.

As best practices, we do well to adopt for our own approach to negotiations, whether informal as in everyday life, or formal and contractual, Abraham's "clear, firm, and polite" approach, along with best practices advocated by those associated with entities such as the Harvard Negotiation Project,

CHAPTER 3
Conciliation: Esau and Jacob

Genesis 32-33

ANCIENT HEADLINES
(as they might have appeared in today's media)

Twin Brothers in Struggle Over Inheritance

Planned Murder Foiled by Running Away

Gifts Sent to Win Brother's Favor

Brothers' Surprising Meeting on Border of Country

TODAY'S HEADLINES
(as they have appeared in today's media)

...Paul extends olive branch by sending Heather caring note
The Mirror (London, England), February 15, 2008

Israel makes preparations to quit peace talks, Arafat sends flowers
AP Online, October 21, 1998

Olive branch thrown by industry on import fight
WWD, January 15, 1985

NKorea's Kim using gifts to win support
AP Online, June 24, 2009

As I was reading the December 1, 2003, *Deccan Chronicle* in Shamshabad-Hyderabad while on a teaching assignment in India, my eyes were drawn to a column headlined "A Girl with Flowers." The column was written by national journalist M.J. Akbar, who had been captivated by a story told by former U.S. President Bill Clinton at a reception in New Delhi hosted by India's then Prime Minister Atal Behari Vajpayee. Clinton, who was visiting India, spun out a tale from his recent presidency.

In the Israeli political campaign leading to the election of 2001 between then Israeli Prime Minister Ehud Barak and his challenger, Ariel Sharon, Clinton became aware of Sharon's intention to make a political statement by visiting the Muslim Noble Sanctuary, called by Jews the Temple Mount, which contains the al-Aqsa Mosque and the Dome of the Rock, among the most holy of Islamic sites. Sharon's politically motivated visit was ill-advised, in President Clinton's view, with the potential for violence. Clinton then called Israeli Prime Minister Barak and advised him to stop Sharon from proceeding with the visit. Barak, in turn, responded that he could not legally do so, and did not have the persuasive power to convince Sharon otherwise. Clinton, then, followed with another suggestion: "First, ensure that there are enough policemen to prevent any violence. Then ask a young Palestinian girl, alone, to wait for Sharon with a bouquet of flowers in her hand. She should give him the flowers, and add one sentence: 'You are most welcome to come here every day when there is peace.'" Clinton believed, as Akbar continued, "that single image would have etched a place in the heart of the region and the mind of the world; it would have defined the future." But that did not happen, and the predicted violence followed.

Clinton himself, ironically, was the recipient of flowers when he later traveled to North Korea in August of 2009 to negotiate the release of two detained American journalists. As he deplaned in Pyongyang, he was welcomed by a young North Korean girl with a large, beautiful bouquet of flowers.

Winning the favor of another through a gift such as flowers is best called conciliation, as distinguished from the fuller transaction of reconciliation. In Genesis we see conciliation modeled by Jacob, whose gifts on the occasion of his homecoming after twenty years in exile quite exceeded a simple bouquet of flowers, but with similar intent. He sought to win the favor of his brother, who earlier had threatened to kill him.

The Story

We begin at the point in the story where Isaac's mother, Sarah, died at the age of 127. Isaac was thirty-seven years old, and was yet unmarried.

A short time after Mother Sarah's death, Father Abraham sent his servant back to his home country to find a wife for Isaac. Among the relatives back home, the servant found a willing young woman named Rebecca and brought her back with him. So at the age of forty, Isaac married Rebecca. We are not given Rebecca's age.

Though the marriage was consummated, twenty years of childlessness followed. History was repeating itself, and one can only imagine what Abraham must have been thinking. Again, it would seem, God was testing his faith, for he was still living, but the text is silent.

Finally, in desperation, Isaac appealed to God on behalf of Rebecca, and Rebecca became pregnant. But this pregnancy quickly became difficult. Rigorous movement in the womb left Rebecca perplexed and distressed. It wasn't until God revealed to her that she, in fact, had two nations inside of her, did she understand. She was pregnant with twins, and already they were struggling with each other. Conflict between them, which was later to escalate, seemed to begin already in the womb.

The twins – Esau and Jacob – were born when father Isaac was sixty years of age. Grandfather Abraham, still living, was 160. The twins were fifteen years old when their grandfather died at the age of 175.

Now Esau, the elder, since he had emerged first from the womb, and Jacob, the younger, were very different types. In recent history, this difference became the text – "My brother Esau was an hairy man, but I am a smooth man" – for the sermon, "Take a Pew," in the brilliant and now classic 1960s British satirical revue titled *Beyond the Fringe*. This text, which begins the sermon, is followed by a series of non-sequiturs, only to return again at the end to the text, as though all that has been spoken in between has illuminated the text, when in fact none of it has had anything to do with the text. A satire of perhaps at least some preaching.

Esau, indeed, was hairy, Jacob was smooth. Esau was a man of the field, Jacob a man of the tent. Esau was father's favorite, Jacob was mother's favorite.

Sibling rivalry is at the heart of this story, and inheritance is again a prominent issue. Esau had the edge, since he was first from the womb. But returning from an unsuccessful hunt one day, and famished, he encountered his brother conveniently stirring up a bowl of lentil soup. Jacob quickly saw an opportunity, and so in response to Esau's plea for some soup, he offered Esau a deal. He would give him some of his soup in exchange for his brother's "birthright," his privileged position as the elder of the two in regard to inheritance. Esau, famished as he was, quickly agreed, and the deal was struck.

Years later, when Father Isaac had passed the age of 130 and was nearly blind, he determined that it was time to bestow the final, privileged blessing on his oldest and favorite son before he died. Esau and Jacob at the time were already in their seventies, no longer young children. The stakes were high.

Arrangements were made by father Isaac with Esau, but were countered by the conniving of mother Rebecca with Jacob. Jacob was secretly dressed with animal skins covering his exposed arms and hands so if felt by his blind father, he would be hairy as his brother Esau. In the absence of his brother, who was out on the hunt at the request of his father for his favorite venison, Jacob then presented himself to his father as Esau. Father Isaac was at first skeptical of the voice, which he perceived to be Jacob's. His touch of the animal skins and the accompanying smell of the field, nevertheless, overpowered his sense of hearing, and he judged that the person before him was indeed his oldest son. So the blessing he intended for Esau he instead bestowed on Jacob.

Learning that Jacob had tricked their father, Esau was enraged. The struggle which began in the womb now exploded in full force. Esau now summarized the past seventy plus years of living together in two principal injustices: "He took away my birthright, and look, now he has taken away my blessing."

"Esau hated Jacob," we are told, and determined to pursue the Cain pathway and kill his brother. With apparent respect for his father, nevertheless, he decided to wait until his father had first died. He "said to himself, 'The days of mourning for my father are approaching; then I will kill my brother Jacob'."

Mother Rebecca, aware of Esau's intention, advised Jacob that it might be best if he would leave for a time. She, moreover, manipulated the situation so that his leaving would be legitimated by her husband. Her strategy was to play on the conflict over marriage in the family. Esau, at the age of forty, had married local Hittite women, who had "made life bitter for Isaac and Rebekah." Jacob, though in his seventies, had not yet married. Rebekah's ruse was to make an issue of Jacob's marriage with her husband, leading him to use marriage as the reason for sending Jacob back to the home country to Rebekah's family in search of a wife. On the surface, Jacob's leaving was given legitimacy, but the underlying motive was to "run away" given Esau's threat of killing his brother.

Back in the home country, Jacob moved in with his uncle Laban, his mother's brother. Here he lived for some twenty years. During this time he did marry. He acquired two wives, both daughters of Uncle Laban, and two "concubines" or secondary wives, each of which produced children. And he became independently wealthy. Jacob's life was radically transformed during this twenty-year span between his early seventies and nineties.

Jacob's life with Uncle Laban, however, was not free of conflict. A variety of conflicts occurred, most of which were resolved through negotiation. Though our Genesis storyteller gives us more details of these conflicts and how they were resolved, it is in what followed his twenty years at his uncle's that we see the new pathway of conciliation emerge. We move, then, to the end of the story.

Our Genesis storyteller informs us that after twenty years at Uncle Laban's, Jacob was instructed by God to return home. That presented a challenge, for going home would not be easy given the circumstances under which he had left. Acceptance at home was no assured matter. Would Esau's earlier intention to kill him now be enacted? What would happen when these two older twin brothers, now in their nineties, again met? We turn now to this part of the story.

The Homecoming

Upon nearing home with his now large family, including his four wives, eleven sons, at least one daughter, and much wealth, Jacob cautiously prepared to meet his brother. His first move was to send an advance delegation to inform Esau of his coming. His intention in doing so was to win Esau's favor. The delegation was instructed by Jacob to say to Esau:

> Thus says your servant Jacob, "I have lived with Laban as an alien, and stayed until now; and I have oxen, donkeys, flocks, male and female slaves; and I have sent to tell my lord, *in order that I may find favor in your sight.*"

Thus he provided Esau with a brief sketch of his time away and his purpose in alerting him to his homecoming—"I have sent to tell my lord, in order that I may find favor in your sight."

The delegation delivered the message, and returned with the report that Esau was on his way to meet Jacob, and with him were 400 men. "Jacob," we are told, "was greatly afraid and distressed." But there was still time to strategize further. First, he divided his people and animals into two companies, thinking that should Esau attack one, the other might escape. In desperation, he then prayed, including this plea: "Deliver me, please, from the hand of my brother, from the hand of Esau, for I am afraid of him; he may come and kill us all, the mothers with the children."

Jacob also put feet to his prayer. He arranged for another diplomatic mission to Esau, but this time he also sent gifts; indeed, a remarkable array of gifts quite beyond a bouquet of flowers: "two hundred female goats and twenty male goats, two hundred ewes and twenty rams, thirty milch camels and their colts, forty cows and ten bulls, twenty female donkeys and ten male donkeys." These he organized in a parade of droves that Esau would meet in succession. A servant was placed in charge of each, and each was instructed to say upon Esau's inquiry as to whose these were: "They belong to your servant Jacob; they are a present sent to my lord Esau; and moreover he is behind us."

Our omniscient storyteller climaxes this episode of the story by again pointing to Jacob's motivation: "For he thought, 'I may appease him with the present that goes ahead of me, and afterwards I shall see his face; perhaps he will accept me'." Again, Jacob's motive of winning his brother's favor is emphasized.

Having sent this delegation with gifts on their way, it was now time for Jacob to prepare himself and his family for the actual meeting with his brother. Camped, as they were, by a stream called Jabbok on the frontier of the homeland, he proceeded that night to move his family and all that he had across the stream. Jacob, however, stayed alone for the remainder of the night on the now vacated side.

Sleep the night before a major meeting of protagonists can be difficult. Even those who seek to mediate between protagonists find it so. Former U.S. President Bill Clinton, for one, reports that he could not go back to sleep after awakening at three in the morning the night before his historic meeting at the White House on September 13, 1993, with Israeli Prime Minister Yitzhak Rabin and Palestinian leader Yasser Arafat. Not being able to sleep, he got up and read through the entire biblical book of Joshua as he waited for dawn. For the day, then, he chose to wear a "blue tie with golden horns," which, he said, "reminded me of those Joshua had used to blow down the walls of Jericho."[1] President Clinton, however, was not alone in being awake that night. Dennis Ross, his envoy to the Middle East, reports that he was up the whole night before together with the protagonists, who continued to wrestle over details of the meeting the next day.[2]

For Jacob, the night before meeting his brother was not only one of wrestling with sleep. His night was invaded by a mysterious stranger, with whom he physically wrestled until dawn. When the match appeared to be a draw, the stranger struck Jacob's hip putting it "out of joint." With dawn then approaching, the stranger insisted on leaving, but Jacob demanded a blessing before he would let him go. A blessing was given, which included a renaming: "You shall no longer be called Jacob, but Israel, for you have striven with God and with humans, and have prevailed." Jacob, concluding that he had "seen God face to face" in the stranger of the night, marveled that he was still alive.

But alive he was, though handicapped by a limp as he began the day he would meet his brother and his 400 men. But there were things he could yet do. In further preparation, Jacob now organized his family into a succession of four mother groups, each with the children she had borne to Jacob. He placed Rachel, his favorite wife, together with their son Joseph, the last to be born at uncle Laban's, at the rear, so the last to be killed, if it came to that. Then he placed himself at the head as the drum major of a parade.

When Esau finally appeared on the horizon, Jacob limped toward him, bowing seven times to the ground as he approached, as one would to an Eastern ruler of the time. Esau, on the other hand, ran to meet him, threw his arms around him, and kissed him, reminiscent of the behavior of the father in Jesus's later story of the homecoming of the prodigal son. Then Esau and Jacob both wept.

But unlike Jesus's later "prodigal son" story of reconciliation between father and son, this story ends differently, as revealed in the subsequent conversation between Esau and Jacob. Esau began the conversation by asking about the family – "Who are these with you?" – and then about the meaning of all the droves of animals with their herdsmen which he had met on the way. His intention, Jacob explained, was "to find favor with my lord," again reinforcing his conciliatory motive as earlier noted. Esau responded, "I have enough, my brother; keep what you have for yourself." But Jacob was not easily deterred. "No, please," he said, "if I find favor with you, then accept my present from my hand; for truly to see your face is like seeing the face of God—since you have received me with such favor. Please accept my gift that is brought to you, because God has dealt graciously with me, and because I have everything I want." So Jacob pressed his conciliatory case, and Esau accepted.

In turn, Esau now made some offers. "Let us journey on our way," he said to Jacob, "and I will go alongside you." Jacob, like Esau, too offered objections. His objections centered on the nature and condition of his family and flocks, which required them to move slowly. In contrast, Esau was traveling lightly. But he added a promise that he would come to Esau at his home in Seir at his own pace.

In conversation with Bill Moyers in his U.S. public television series on Genesis, Old Testament scholar Walter Brueggeman noted that "the very last thing Jacob does is lie to his brother. He says, 'I'll meet you,' and then he goes the other way."[3] The subsequent account reveals that instead of heading south to Seir where Esau lived, he went the opposite direction to Succoth.

But Esau tried again. He made another offer. "Let me leave with you some of the people who are with me," he suggested to Jacob. But Jacob turned down the offer. He saw no need for it. So they parted, heading in opposite directions in spite of what Jacob had promised.

Whereas some interpreters have suggested that these two brothers were reconciled with each other, a close examination of their final interaction suggests otherwise. For one, the ability to give and receive gifts provides a clue as to how the relationship was perceived by the two brothers. Jacob gave, but refused to receive. Esau, on the other hand, was able to both give and receive. For Jacob the relationship was not yet equal.

Robert Alter, Hebrew scholar and translator of Genesis, adds this observation: "Clearly, he [Jacob] is declining the offer of Esau's retainers because he still doesn't trust Esau and intends to put a large distance between himself and Esau or any of Esau's men."[4]

A close examination of word choice further illuminates the subtleties of the verbal dance between the two brothers. Jacob consistently refers to his brother as "my lord," never to the end breaking out of this hierarchical language. Indeed, as Robert Alter has pointed out, the last words in this verbal exchange in the Hebrew text are Jacob's words to Esau, "my lord."[5] On the other hand, from beginning to end Esau addresses Jacob as "my brother," the language of family and familiarity. Jacob's language keeps his brother Esau at arm's length.

Then there is Jacob's purpose in this encounter. Throughout the story from beginning to end, Jacob's goal is repeatedly noted as winning his brother Esau's favor— "to find favor with my lord." The dominant Hebrew word Jacob uses to explain his motivation is *chen,* usually translated as favor or grace. Only once in this narrative does Jacob use the Hebrew *nasa',* which is sometimes translated as forgiveness, and then it occurs only as a private thought. In explaining his motivation to Esau in their final conversation, Jacob consistently uses *chen;* that is, to gain his brother's favor.

I conclude, then, that what occurred between Esau and Jacob in this narrative was not reconciliation. Conciliation more accurately describes what happened between these brothers. This is not to diminish the significance of what happened, for winning the favor of another can be of great value, perhaps even keep one from being killed.

Conciliation Today

Conciliation, in everyday, ordinary language, as defined by Webster, means "to gain favor, to win over, soothe the anger of; make friendly; placate… by friendly acts." That, precisely, was Jacob's goal in his homecoming. This goal, though short of reconciliation, is often, nevertheless, quite useful. Indeed, gaining another's favor, beyond reducing tensions, may also produce other benefits. It may even make it possible to bury a father together, as Esau and Jacob later united in burying their father, who lived much longer than apparently he thought he would. Father Isaac died at the age of 180, quite beyond Jacob's homecoming. In reporting this joint burial, our Genesis narrator interestingly reverts back to their birth order: "…his sons Esau and Jacob buried him."

Conciliation has several synonyms as in pacify or appease. To speak of appeasing, however, tends to evoke negative connotations, perhaps particularly because of its failure during the 1930s to stop Hitler. Yet conciliation, whether called appeasement or otherwise, is common among us. A husband who appears with a rose for his wife after a bitter exchange is engaged in conciliation. Likewise, a son who seeks the pleasure of a parent after a tense argument in order to obtain the keys to the family car is similarly engaged; or an employee, who see things very differently than her employer and yet seeks the favor of her employer in order to obtain other benefits. Even the more powerful who wish to retain the support of subordinates who are yet needed, may conciliate or appease by granting certain benefits that otherwise might not be granted.

Conciliation is a strategy, too, of nations. Indeed, the story of Esau and Jacob itself has political overtones. Mother Rebecca's difficult pregnancy, it may be remembered, was interpreted as the presence of two nations in her womb. From Esau came Edom, and from Jacob,

Israel – two nations of the ancient world who later had their own conflicts, extensions of their two fathers.

In modern times, the birth of the United States itself was surrounded by a debate over conciliation, climaxed by Edmund Burke's great speech in England's House of Commons on "Conciliation of the American Colonies." Had Burke's powerful arguments for conciliation been heeded, the history of Britain and the United States might have been quite different. But England chose the path of coercive power, which produced its own counterforce in the American Revolution.

More recently, appeasement of Hitler during the 1930s, as I have noted, has given the term a bad press. "Appeasement" has taken on the character of a "devil term," to use the language of mid-twentieth-century rhetorician Richard M. Weaver. Realities so labeled are automatically viewed as negative. Yet more thoughtful analyses of the virtues and liabilities of appeasement suggest a more nuanced response. As Geoffrey Wheatcroft has written, "There is by now an entire book to be written about the way that 'Munich,' 'appeasement,' and 'Churchill' have been ritually invoked, from Suez to Vietnam to Iraq, so often in false analogy, and so often with calamitous results."[6]

A book which would include positive examples of appeasement-conciliation would surely include the story of the American-Soviet missile crisis of 1962. We now know that the world came as close to nuclear war as we ever have in the confrontation between the United States and the Soviet Union over its strategy of installing missiles at the time in Cuba. President John F. Kennedy took a firm stand insisting that the Soviet Union remove the missiles, leading to a tense stand-off that had the possibility of escalating into nuclear war. Finally, on a Sunday morning, October 28, 1962, word reached the White House that Krushchev was withdrawing the Soviet missiles. Theodore Sorenson, advisor to President Kennedy, describes the instructions the president then gave to his team. "He laid down the line we were all to follow—no boasting, no gloating, not even a claim of victory. We had won by enabling Khruschev to avoid complete humiliation—we should not humiliate him now...." Then, "rejecting the temptation of a dramatic TV appearance," Kennedy "issued a brief three-paragraph statement welcoming Khrushchev's 'statesmanlike decision...an important and constructive contribution to peace,' " followed by a conciliatory letter to the Soviet Chairman applauding his "firm undertakings."[7]

While we now know more of the complexities that actually shaped actions of the time, President Kennedy, nevertheless, seems to have learned the art of balancing firmness with conciliation. Linked together, they became a powerful force that helped to improve the relationship between the United States and the Soviet Union. It was not reconciliation, but this experience, linked to other simultaneous and also future conciliatory moves of the Kennedy administration, led to better relations between these two, principal competing nations of the time.

In brief, then, from the ancient world of Esau and Jacob to our modern families, organizations and communities, and from ancient nations such as Edom (Esau) and Israel (Jacob) to the modern nations of the Middle East as well as the rest of the world, conciliation remains a useful strategy. It can help to reduce tensions—between family members, between neighbors, between groups, and between nations, and perhaps at times even keep us from killing each other. The challenge is to know when to stand firm and when to conciliate, or simultaneously do both. Wisdom is to discern which strategy at which time may best move us forward toward a just peace.

BEST PRACTICE
Conciliation

In the late 1960s, I participated in a week-long Institute for Advanced Pastoral Studies in Berkeley, California. Though not a pastor, I was privileged to attend since I was including the leader in a doctoral dissertation I was working on at the time.

Toward the end of the week, we engaged in a communion (Eucharist, Lord's Supper) service organized in a manner akin to a tribal event, appropriate to the 1960s. Toward the end of the event, we engaged in a free-wheeling "dance," taking each others' hands, as we twirled with this and that partner around the room. In the process, I reached out to an older pastor, and for a moment the two of us swung together.

In a later reflection on this experience, this older pastor, who in the earlier week had expressed frustration over his inability to relate to younger parishioners in this challenging time, acknowledged that he had been uncertain about how I felt toward him given that I had said some challenging things to him. But when I took the initiative to reach out to him in that communion service, though unaware of his feelings, his doubts went away. Perhaps there was more than conciliation that happened here, but reaching out to the other with hope that the other will respond positively is the essence of conciliation. It can even happen when not aware of the other's feelings, as in my 1960's experience. For Jacob in our story, it was extravagant gifts that he hoped would positively impact his brother's feelings toward him. For others, as in more recent examples, it may be an unexpected bouquet of flowers. For others it might be a kind note or a kind deed. The possibilities are many. Not all conflicts are immediately resolvable. They sometimes require first reaching out to the other in ways that rebuild a relationship so mutual problem solving can follow. Conciliation can then become a best practice on our pathway to peace.

CHAPTER 4
Genocide: Dinah and Her Brothers

Genesis 34

ANCIENT HEADLINES
(as they might have appeared in today's media)

Prince Negotiates for Hand of Local Nomad After Rape

Circumcision Agreed to as Price for Bride

Surprise Slaughter of Local Villagers

Brothers of Intended Bride Identified as Killers

TODAY'S HEADLINES
(as they have appeared in today's media)

Massacre in Bosnia; Srebrenica: The Days of Slaughter
The New York Times, October 29, 1995

Slaughter on the Isle of Peace
The Independent (London, England), March 14, 1997

Witnesses describe another massacre in southern Darfur
international Herald Tribune, October 28, 2007

Pastor and son guilty of role in Rwanda genocide
The Scotsman, February 20, 2003

The pathway to where peace is at home occasionally takes an unexpected turn. A traumatic event can quickly precipitate such a turn. For Kenyans, such an event was the divisive election of 2007. Post the election, I sat one day in the capital city of Nairobi listening to a group of Christian pastors reflect on the tribal divisions that had surfaced in their multi-tribe city congregations during the election. Cross-tribal marital engagements were being tested, friendships between children of different tribes were strained; and the like. Whatever teachings of peace had occurred in these congregations, they were now being trumped by tribal interests; though, of course, there were also exceptions.

In our story of Dinah and her brothers, the traumatic event was a rape, and the dominating issue was the honor of the family, appropriate to the cultural context of the time. The response to the rape, nevertheless, was similar to responses throughout history as not only family and tribal, but also religious and ethnic identities and honor have challenged those formerly living together in peace.

In ancient Palestine, the patriarchal families of Abraham, Isaac and Jacob lived in separate enclaves from their native neighbors. Inevitably, nevertheless, they could not avoid contact with these neighbors. Though the focus of the Genesis stories is largely on the internal dynamics of these early families, they also include stories that begin to give us clues about relating to neighbors, and sometimes enemies.

What I here call an enclave the mythologist Joseph Campbell has called a "bounded community," or a "bounded field." In a bounded community, as Campbell has observed, "brotherhood," a major theme of Genesis, is reserved for the insider, "aggression is projected outward."[1] The story of the rape of Dinah, the daughter of Jacob and his first wife Leah, provides one example.

Aggression, however, was only one of several ways in which these early families related to outsiders. Deception was another. On two reported occasions, for example, fear drove Abraham and Sarah to use this strategy, as noted in chapter two of this work. Perceiving Sarah's beauty as a danger to Abraham's life, they deceived their "outsider" neighbors by presenting themselves as brother and sister rather than husband and wife. They feared powerful neighbors might kill Abraham to add Sarah to their harems if they knew he was her husband. Isaac and Rebecca, their son and his wife, later used the same strategy for the same reason. In each case this strategy backfired, yet their lives were spared.

Competition with neighbors over scarce water wells produced yet other ways of dealing with neighbors. In Abraham's case, a dispute over a well led to a protest to the ruler of the region, followed by a peaceful resolution. In Isaac, his son's case, he "lumped it," as earlier noted, and simply moved on and dug more wells until he had one that the neighbors did not dispute.

In brief, negotiation, protesting against injustice, deception, "lumping it," and aggression were all ways used by these ancient families to relate to their outsider neighbors. In the foregoing examples, the primary concern was what today we call peace and security.

The story of the rape of Dinah adds the even more basic concern of family honor and shame. Even in present individualistic cultures, honor and shame easily trump peace and security concerns. Psychiatrist James Gilligan has observed, "The death of the self is of far greater concern than the death of the body. People will willingly sacrifice their bodies if they perceive it as the only way to avoid 'losing their souls,' 'losing their minds,' or 'losing face'."[2]

How, then, might we understand this story of the rape of Dinah and the subsequent violence given the seeming progression in Genesis from murder to separation to conciliation, and ultimately to reconciliation, the final story yet to be told? One reality suggested by the story is that when confronted by a major traumatic experience such as rape, a very human temptation is to revert to that first, primal post-Eden pathway of killing the other, regardless of what we have learned along the way. Before moving on to the final story of reconciliation, then, we must deal with this very real and human story of retreat to violence, motivated in this case by the violation of the honor of the family.

The Story

Dinah, as I have noted, was the daughter of Jacob and Leah, the first of his four wives.

Our Genesis storyteller informs us that Dinah "went out to visit the women of the region." She crossed the boundary of her family and tribal identity to visit the "other." While on her visit, Shechem, the son of Hamor, prince of the region, saw her, "seized her and lay with her by force." But his relationship with Dinah was complicated. We are told that he was drawn to her and actually "loved the girl, and spoke tenderly to her." Furthermore, he asked his father, Hamor, to arrange to have Dinah become his wife.

This mix of violence and love "complicates the moral balance of the story," as Hebrew scholar Robert Alter observes.[3] It also opens the door to imaginative retellings such as we have in Anita Diamant's novel, *The Red Tent* (1997), where the story is retold from the perspective of Dinah. In the Genesis account, nevertheless, the point-of-view of the men in the family clearly dominates, reflective of the cultural context. For them, Dinah had been violated, and the honor of the family besmirched.

When Father Jacob heard the news of what had happened, he chose to "hold his peace" until his now grown sons returned from the field, where they were tending the cattle. This simple report marks a change in the dynamics of Jacob's family. As children grow, their voice in family matters also increases.

When the brothers came in from the fields and heard what had happened, we are told that they "were indignant and very angry," because Shechem, the outsider, "had committed an outrage in Israel by lying with Jacob's daughter, for such a thing ought not to be done." Again, as in that first post-Eden story of Cain and Abel, the strong emotions of anger and rage triggered a violent response, though a cleverly planned and premeditated response in the face of a more powerful opponent. The events which led to that violent response now follow.

The protagonists—Hamor and his son, Shechem; and Jacob and his sons—initially met to address the problem. Prince Hamor, who had come to see Jacob at the request of his son, opened the meeting with a marriage proposal:

> The heart of my son Shechem longs for your daughter; please give her to him in marriage. Make marriages with us; give your daughters to us, and take our daughters for yourselves. You shall live with us; and the land shall be open to you; live and trade in it, and get property in it.

Clearly Prince Hamor saw the immediate situation as an opportunity to forge a larger alliance. Shechem, his son, however, was more focused on his immediate concern of marriage, and followed his father's opening proposal with an appeal:

> Let me find favor with you, and whatever you say to me I will give. Put the marriage present and gift as high as you like, and I will give whatever you ask me; only give me the girl to be my wife.

Father Jacob did not respond. He was supplanted by his angry sons, who responded "deceitfully, because he had defiled their sister Dinah." Family honor, for them, took precedence over all else. So they replied:

> We cannot do this thing, to give our sister to one who is uncircumcised, for that would be a disgrace to us. Only on

this condition will we consent to you: that you will become as we are and every male among you be circumcised. Then we will give our daughters to you, and we will take your daughters for ourselves, and we will live among you and become one people. But if you will not listen to us and be circumcised, then we will take our daughter and be gone.

We are not told whether Father Jacob participated in creating this response. Given what followed, however, we can surmise that he was not aware of his sons' fuller intentions.

Prince Hamor and his son were "pleased" with the proposal. Shechem moved quickly to implement these demands, "because he was delighted with Jacob's daughter." Shechem was in a good position to proceed, furthermore, inasmuch as he "was the most honored of all his family," apparently having earned the respect of his people. So Hamor and his son met with the men of their city at the city gate, and presented their case:

These people are friendly with us; let them live in the land and trade in it, for the land is large enough for them; let us take their daughters in marriage, and let us give them our daughters. Only on this condition will they agree to live among us, to become one people: that every male among us be circumcised as they are circumcised. Will not their livestock, their property, and all their animals be ours? Only let us agree with them, and they will live among us.

Persuaded by this presentation, the men of the city proceeded to be circumcised, not realizing that they were falling into a trap. "On the third day, when they were still in pain," Simeon and Levi, full brothers of Dinah as also children of Leah, took swords, sneaked into the city, and killed all the males, including Prince Hamor and his son, Shechem.

We are then told that Simeon and Levi "took Dinah out of Shechem's house" and left. Robert Alter, citing Meir Sternberg, notes "that this is a shocking revelation just before the end of the story: we might have imagined that Shechem was petitioning in good faith for Dinah's hand; now it emerges that he has been holding her captive in his house after having raped her."[4] The violence of Simeon and Levi was followed by the pillaging of the city, the rest of the brothers also joining in. The motivation for this continuing violence and destruction is again identified by our Genesis storyteller as a matter of honor—"because their sister had been defiled."

It is only after the genocide of the village that we again hear the voice of Father Jacob. He specifically addressed Simeon and Levi, who had led this horrific violence. His reasoning is pragmatic representing peace and security concerns:

> You have brought trouble on me by making me odious to the inhabitants of the land, the Canaanites and the Perezzites; my numbers are few, and if they gather themselves against me and attack me, I shall be destroyed, both I and my household.

The brothers' defense was again one of honor: "Should our sister be treated like a whore?" With this defense the story ends.

The memory of these events, however, continued. But not until years later toward the end of Jacob's life does this memory resurface in the Genesis narrative. Father Jacob was nearing death, now in Egypt where he had moved with his family at the invitation of his son Joseph, who had become a leader in the land. Before his death, Jacob gathered his sons around him for the purpose of telling them what would happen "in days to come." He had a word for each son, but Simeon and Levi, who had led in the Shechem massacre, he linked together. Of them he said:

> Simeon and Levi are brothers;
> weapons of violence are their swords.

> May I never come into their council;
> May I not be joined to their company—
> For in their anger they killed men,
> and at their whim they hamstrung oxen.
> Cursed be their anger, for it is fierce,
> and their wrath, for it is cruel!
> I will divide them in Jacob,
> and scatter them in Israel.

Unlike Jacob's earlier, pragmatic peace and security response, his condemnation now was principled in nature. Jacob will have none of it.

The story thus has this epilogue. By implication, the earlier "no" to violence against a brother is now extended also to the outsider. In noting that "in their anger they killed men," Jacob makes no distinction between insiders and outsiders. As to consequences, Simeon and Levi will be divided in Jacob and scattered in Israel, analogous to Cain's earlier banishment. Choices do have consequences.

Nevertheless, we are still left with a question. If I am my sister's keeper, what does Jacob propose as an appropriate alternative to violence in situations such as rape? Surely such violations are not to be excused and overlooked. But Jacob is silent beyond condemning the violence. Yet knowing what is not acceptable is at least a beginning.

Jacob, simultaneously, did have further experiences with sexual deviation. It happened within his own family. Reuben, his oldest son, was guilty. He had had sexual intercourse with Bilhah, one of Jacob's secondary wives. So in his last words to his sons before he died, he also had a word for Reuben:

> Reuben, you are my firstborn,
> My might and the first fruits of my vigor,
> Excelling in rank and excelling in power.
> Unstable as water, you shall no longer excel
> Because you went up onto your father's bed;

Then you defiled it—you went up onto my couch!

In this situation, again there were consequences—"you shall no longer excel," or be first as the oldest, as it has also been translated.

Then there was also Judah, Jacob's fourth son by Leah, his first wife. Judah, too, had his sexual challenges. His story is told in the thirty-eighth chapter of Genesis.

Like his sister Dinah, Judah also chose to cross the boundary of family and tribe and consort with outsiders. He not only became a friend with a Canaanite named Hireh, but also married a Canaanite woman named Shua, with whom he had three sons: Er, Onan and Shelah.

When Er, the oldest, came of age, he married Tamar, who became a widow when "the Lord put him to death" because of his wickedness. Onan, the second oldest, was then instructed by his father to "perform the duty of a brother-in-law" by raising up children for his brother by having sexual intercourse with widow Tamar, as was the custom of the time. But he refused. Rather, "he spilled his semen on the ground whenever he went in to his brother's wife..." This, too, displeased God, and Onan died. This left Shelah, the youngest, who was not yet of age. Judah, nevertheless, promised Shelah to Tamar when he would come of age.

Within time, Shuah, the wife of Judah, also died, leaving him a widower. When Shelah came of age, Judah did not follow through with his earlier promise to Tamar. So Tamar created a plan to catch his attention. She disguised herself as a prostitute, and offered herself to Judah for a price at a convenient juncture along a road he traveled. He accepted. Not having payment in hand, he gave her his signet, cord and staff as a pledge for later payment. However, when Judah sent payment, she could not be found, having shed her disguise.

Upon hearing that Tamar had played the role of a prostitute and become pregnant, Judah was outraged and demanded that she be burned. But the signet, cord and staff, now produced by Tamar, proved that he, in fact, was the guilty one who had made her pregnant.

Now that Tamar had gotten Judah's attention and he had been found guilty, what would he do? Would he be further enraged because he had been tricked and embarrassed, and perhaps order an even hotter fire for her burning? It is at moments such as this that one's deeper character is revealed. To his credit, Judah acknowledged: "She is more in the right than I, since I did not give her to my son Shelah." Tamar subsequently gave birth to twins named Perez and Zerah. Though born to an outsider mother, they figure significantly in the genealogy of ancient Israel (e.g. Ruth 4:12; 1 Chronicles 2:4; Matthew 1:3).

Judah's ability to acknowledge his error and accept responsibility for what had happened, even though he had lost face, are noteworthy. Unlike Cain, Simeon and Levi, Judah was able to turn from his anger and own his error. This introduction to Judah is significant, for it presages a similar cycle in the last Genesis story of Joseph and his brothers, as we shall see.

The Mass Murder of Genocide

The story of Raphael Lemkin's twentieth century journey to convince the world community to name mass murder as "genocide" is told by Samantha Power in her Pulitzer Prize winning book, *"A Problem From Hell": America and the Age of Genocide* (2002). On December 9, 1948, after years of persistent efforts on Lemkin's part, the United Nations General Assembly finally and unanimously passed a law banning genocide.

Earlier that year, the Convention on the Prevention and Punishment of the Crime of Genocide had defined it as follows:

> Any of the following acts committed with intent to destroy, in whole or in part, a national, ethnical, racial, or religious group, as such:
> A. Killing members of the group;
> B. Causing serious bodily or mental harm to members of the group;

C. Deliberately inflicting on the group the conditions of life calculated to bring about its physical destruction in whole or in part;
D. Imposing measures intended to prevent births within the group;
E. Forcibly transferring children of the group to another group.[5]

What happened in ancient Shechem qualifies as genocide under this definition. Unfortunately, neither legal definitions and laws or religious and moral values have been sufficient in either the ancient or modern world to prevent genocides. These have been trumped by perceived violations of honor of both family and tribe, as well as nations.

In our time, the genocide of Shechem has been a repeated experience. Indeed, as "murder [did] not really come into its own until the twentieth century," so genocide, too, could be viewed as not having really come into its own until the twentieth century. Samantha Power's title for her book, "*A Problem From Hell*", rings with realism. Names of places in her chapter titles indicate the breadth of the problem: Cambodia, Iraq, Bosnia, Rwanda, Srebrenica, Kosovo. So added to ancient Shechem has been a growing list of villages, towns and countries who have experienced the mass murder of genocide. Simultaneously, added to the ancient voice of Jacob have been other voices, including the United Nations in our time, who have said "no" to such violence. But the challenge remains as paths are strewn with rape, torture, beheadings, massacres, and the most unimaginable of human violations.

In response, personal journeys are also instructive. In ancient times, Judah's capacity to turn his first impulse to burn his daughter-in-law Tamar into self reflection, recognizing his own contribution to the problem, is significant. In our time, theologian Miroslav Volf, as a son of Croatia, has courageously narrated his own journey toward a theology that embraces rather than excludes in the face of the violence against his own people during the 1990s in the Balkan conflicts.⁶

Finally, I return to the resolute voice of Jacob himself, who long before the United Nations took action to ban genocide, moved from pragmatism to principle, and so declared:

> Simeon and Levi are brothers;
> weapons of violence are their swords.
> May I never come into their council;
> May I not be joined to their company....

BEST PRACTICE
Transcendent Values

Cain had his issue with Abel, his brother. But in our story in this chapter, Jacob's sons took it to another level leading to genocide.

What Jacob's sons forgot in the heat of their anger was the transcendent teaching of their tradition that all humankind are created in the image of God. For myself as an American, that truth was likewise enshrined at the beginning of my nation: All persons, as we would say today, "are created equal and...endowed by their Creator with certain unalienable Rights, that among these are Life, Liberty and the pursuit of Happiness."

When tempted to wipe out a people as in genocide, a best practice is to remember and trumpet this transcendent value of both creation and country.

But even when faced with a lesser evil, remembering such a transcendent value counters the seed of exclusion that has the potential of leading to genocide.

My own experience bears witness. Beginning with the fifth grade, my childhood home was in a small, central California valley town. After moving from the Midwest in 1945, my carpenter father built us a home in a newly opened development which prohibited "any Negro, Japanese, Hindu, Armenian, Malayan, native of the Turkish Empire,

Mexican, Chinese, Korean, or any person not of the Caucasian race, or descendant of above named persons…" from living in this development. Furthermore, being within a town block of my local, denominational church, the church also built its parsonage in this same development. And from this segregated housing development, the pastor, ironically, was called to a leadership position in the global mission organization of the denomination. So while singing in church that Jesus loves all the children of the world, "red, yellow, black and white," most of the children of the world were excluded from living on my street. While neither my family nor my denomination's local church created this restriction, neither also did nothing to remove it. It took the United States government to do that, finally acting on its own transcendent value that all people are created equal and are entitled to equal access to housing.

The global mission of my church was rooted in the belief that all people need to come to know Jesus as their Savior and Lord. But somehow, that didn't seem to register as relevant to who lived in my neighborhood. So we participated in what today we would call systemic racism.

Transcendent values are only as good as they are practiced. When called upon, whether during divisive times or otherwise, advocating for their relevance is essential.

CHAPTER 5
Reconciliation: Joseph and His Brothers

Genesis 37-50

ANCIENT HEADLINES
(as they might have appeared in today's media)

Local Boy Sold Into Slavery by Brothers

Slave Charged With Attempted Rape

Prisoner Appointed Second-In-Command in Land

Country Leader and Brothers Reconcile

TODAY'S HEADLINES
(as they have appeared in today's media)

Forgiveness a difficult virtue
Hindustan Times (New Delhi, India), November 7, 2005

Why the Amish forgive so quickly
The Christian Science Monitor, October 2, 2007

Father, daughter reconcile through letters
Deseret News (Salt Lake City), September 7, 2005)

Truth and reconciliation commissions: instruments for ending impunity and building lasting peace
UN Chronicle, December 1, 2004

Upon arriving for a short visit to India in early 1999, my wife and I witnessed a nation seeking to come to terms with a gruesome murder. On the night of January 22-23, Graham Staines, Australian Christian missionary and social worker, together with his two sons, Phillip, ten, and Timothy, seven, had been burned alive in their old Willy's station wagon where they had retired for the night while visiting the village of Manoharpur in the state of Orissa. A radical Hindu mob opposed to Christian conversions had poured gas on the wagon and set it on fire, blocking any attempts to escape.

The murder of Graham and his sons quickly became a national news story. *India Today*, the country's leading English language news magazine, featured the three on the front cover of the February 8, 1999, issue. Newspapers across the country carried the story. The shame of what had happened, moreover, caused political and religious leaders alike, along with journalists, to strongly condemn it.

The response of Gladys Staines, now widow of Graham, who together with daughter Esther had not been present on that fateful night in the village, was even more powerful. As reported in the Indian press, "Gladys issued a moving statement, forgiving those who murdered her husband and two minor sons." In an op-ed piece which followed, Indian journalist Sushil J. Aaron challenged that "if the Christian aspiration in India is to rouse the conscience of this nation, then it should follow the path shown by Gladys Staines."[1]

The path to forgiveness is sometimes short and at other times long. For Gladys Staines it was short, though even when short it remains a continuing journey. For Joseph and his brothers in our final Genesis story, it took nearly forty years.

The path to forgiveness, moreover, is sometimes one-sided as the person harmed simply extends forgiveness to the other without consideration for an apology or plea to be forgiven. So it was with Gladys. Her response was not contingent on the response of the offenders. In the story of Joseph and his brothers, however, we have a model of forgiveness that leads also to reconciliation, which inevitably must be two-sided.

We turn, then, to this final story of the quest of earth's first families to find their way to where peace is at home. As other of these ancient stories of Genesis, the story of Joseph and his brothers, too, has sparked the imagination of novelists, artists and musicians over the ages. More recently, Andrew Lloyd Webber's musical, *Joseph and his Amazing Technicolor Dreamcoat,* has become a popular retelling of the story, though "technicolor" is a quite imaginative translation of ancient Hebrew. Popular as modern retellings may be, we return, nevertheless, to the account as we find it in the Hebrew Bible.

The Story

Joseph was the first of two sons of Jacob by Rachel, his favorite wife. Among all twelve sons by Jacob's four wives, he was the second youngest; Benjamin, his full brother, was the youngest. Joseph was Jacob's favorite son.

The story begins with Joseph at the age of seventeen. He then began to shepherd in the fields with his older brothers, and "brought a bad report of them to their father." What the brothers were doing in the field is not reported, though this did not keep Jewish rabbis of old from speculating. Rabbi Meir suggested that Joseph reported to his father: "Your sons are … eating limbs cut from living beasts." Rabbi Judah suggested: "They insult the sons of the handmaidens [secondary wives] and they call them slaves." Rabbi Simeon suggested: "They stare at the daughters of the land"[2] Whatever the report, it did not endear Joseph to his brothers. It was a strike against him.

Father Jacob's preferential love for Joseph was demonstrated one day through a special gift of "a long robe with sleeves," what Webber imaginatively calls "His Amazing Technicolor Dreamcoat." Whether technicolor or not, the coat was special. For Joseph's brothers, the coat was evidence that "their father loved him more than all his brothers," and "they hated him, and could not speak peaceably to him." Another strike against him.

The relationship between Joseph and his brothers was further strained by his dreams, which he did not have the good sense to keep to himself. One dream had his brothers' sheaves in the field bowing down to his sheaf, which further intensified their hatred for him. In another dream, the sun, moon and eleven stars bowed down to him, which caused even his father to rebuke him, given the obvious meaning that not only his eleven brothers, but also his father as sun and mother as moon would bow down to him. Still another strike against him.

The brothers believed in the "three strikes and you're out" approach to justice. So one day when Joseph's father again sent him to check on his sons and the flocks they were tending in a distant field, the brothers saw their opportunity for revenge.

When the brothers saw him coming wearing his special "long robe with sleeves," they quickly huddled in the field to plot their revenge. Their first thought was to kill him, and so walk the Cain path. Reuben, the oldest, opposed killing him. "Let us not take his life," Reuben said. "Shed no blood; throw him into this pit here in the wilderness, but lay no hand on him." His plan was later to "rescue him out of their hand and restore him to his father."

The brothers yielded to Reuben, and proceeded to strip Joseph of his special robe and throw him into the pit. We are then told that the brothers sat down to eat, while Reuben apparently watched the flocks at some distance. As they ate, they saw a caravan of Ishmaelite traders approaching on their way to Egypt. The sight of the caravan created another opportunity, and so again they consulted among themselves. In the absence of Reuben, Judah, the fourth son of Jacob, took the lead. "Why not sell him to these Ishmaelites?" he said to his brothers. "Let us do him no harm, for after all, he is our brother, our own flesh and blood" (REB). And his brothers agreed.

Judah's moral reasoning resurfaces the brother theme of Genesis. "Am I my brother's keeper?" Well, yes, he seems to reason. I really shouldn't kill my brother, my own flesh and blood, but he is a bother. So why not get rid of him in another way, the way of "forced separation," as I have called it in examining the separation pathways of Abraham's family.

They then made a deal with the Ishmaelite traders, selling Joseph into slavery for twenty pieces of silver. So they were rid of their irritating brother, who now was on his way to distant Egypt.

Reuben later returned to the pit and finding Joseph gone, tore his clothes in distress. What would they now do? What would they tell their father?

The brothers conspired in a cover-up. They dipped Joseph's robe in the blood of a goat, and delivered it to Father Jacob as something they had found on the way. They asked him to identify the robe, and did not correct him when he concluded that Joseph must have been attacked and killed by a wild animal. An ancient "Watergate," or perhaps we might call it a "Goatgate."

In Egypt, Joseph was purchased by Potiphar, the captain of Pharaoh's guard. He served Potiphar well; indeed, so well that within time Potiphar appointed him as the overseer of his house and his entire estate.

What followed in Potiphar's house matches any contemporary soap opera. Being young, "handsome and good-looking," Potiphar's wife was attracted to him, and attempted to seduce him. Joseph resisted, but eventually got caught in a compromising situation when one day Potiphar's wife grabbed his garment as he fled her advances. Frustrated, she turned on him with the charge of attempted rape, with the evidence of his garment in her hand.

Prison time followed, yet again Joseph rose to a leadership role. The chief jailer, within time, placed all the prisoners under his care, which eventually brought him into contact with Pharaoh's chief cupbearer and chief baker. They had been charged with wrongdoing, and as a result, had also been thrown into prison. Perplexing dreams of these two were interpreted by Joseph, and subsequent events validated his interpretation of the dreams. One was declared guilty and executed, and the other innocent and returned to Pharaoh's service.

Sometime later, his ability to interpret dreams came to the attention of Pharaoh himself. Pharaoh had had dreams he could not decipher, nor could any of the wise men of Egypt. Joseph's ability to interpret dreams was then recalled by Pharaoh's servant who earlier had been released from prison. So Joseph was brought from prison to attempt to interpret Pharaoh's strange dreams.

The dreams, as interpreted, forecast seven years of "great plenty" followed by seven years of famine throughout the entire land. For a leader to know what is coming is certainly useful. But Joseph did not stop with just interpreting the dreams. He boldly proceeded to lay out a plan to prepare for what was coming. We are told that "the proposal pleased Pharaoh and all his servants." So impressed was Pharaoh with Joseph that he proceeded to place him in charge of implementing the plan with no one in higher authority other than Pharaoh himself. So Joseph, at the age of thirty, was second in command in the land, reporting directly to Pharaoh himself.

The years between seventeen and thirty were momentous, maturing years for Joseph. From an arrogant rural youth who threw dreams of superiority into the faces of his older brothers and parents, he grew through the depths of slavery and imprisonment, as well as the preparatory leadership roles in Popithar's house and prison, to become the second-in-command of the whole land of Egypt.

What God revealed to Pharaoh through his dreams, as interpreted by Joseph, came to pass. The seven years of plenty passed, and the seven years of famine began. The famine was widespread throughout the ancient world, including Canaan where Joseph's father and family continued to live.

As we now fast forward the story, we find that Father Jacob heard that there was food in Egypt. So he sent his sons to Egypt for food, and, of course, there they encountered their brother, who at first they did not recognize. A series of dramatic encounters followed, which we will return to later. But for now we move to the end of the story.

After finally revealing who he was, Joseph moved his father and brothers to Egypt given that five years of famine remained. There they settled and lived for many years.

Father Jacob was 130 years old when the family moved to Egypt. He died seventeen years later at the age of 147. His death precipitated events that illuminate our last pathway in these Genesis stories for dealing with conflict—the pathway of reconciliation. We turn, now, to an examination of this pathway as it is modeled in the closing episode in the final chapter of the book.

A Model of Reconciliation

Unlike the narratives of the families of Abraham and Isaac, the Jacob family story has a postscript. Each of the prior stories ends with the rival brothers joining together to bury their father. Likewise, Jacob's sons joined together to bury their father. But in the Jacob family story postscript, unresolved conflict between the brothers and Joseph is yet addressed.

With Father Jacob now gone, the brothers were on their own. No longer could they depend on the restraining influence of their father, and so the brothers feared that Joseph might finally take his revenge for what they had done to him, now nearly forty years ago. Being in power, he was in a position to do so. Our storyteller reports:

> Now that their father was dead, Joseph's brothers were afraid, for they said, "What if Joseph should bear a grudge against us and pay us back for all the harm we did to him?" They therefore sent a messenger to Joseph to say, "In his last words to us before he died, your father gave us this message: 'Say this to Joseph: I ask you to forgive your brothers' crime and wickedness; I know they did you harm.' So now we beg you: forgive our crime, for we are servants of your father's God." Joseph was moved to tears by their words. His brothers approached and bowed to the ground before him. "We are

your slaves," they said. But Joseph replied, "Do not be afraid. Am I in the place of God? You meant to do me harm; but God meant to bring good out of it by preserving the lives of many people, as we see today. Do not be afraid. I shall provide for you and your dependents." Thus he comforted them and set their minds at rest (REB).

The death of a parent creates new opportunities. On one hand, there is the opportunity for revenge, as the brothers feared. On the other hand, there is also the opportunity to make right what after nearly forty years has not yet been fully resolved.

In this case, the brothers, fearing for their lives, took the initiative. They first sent a messenger to make their plea, an indirect approach still common in some cultures today. Then they followed in person, reiterating personally the plea sent through the messenger.

It is in this final encounter between the brothers and Joseph that we see a model of reconciliation. Embedded in the encounter are three critical elements of the reconciliation process, though not always ordered sequentially as outlined here.

Confession

The first is that of confession. The brothers acknowledged that they had committed a crime—they had done wrong. They did not equivocate, offer excuses or shift blame, though it had taken them nearly forty years to get to this point. They were guilty, and they not only knew it, but they also clearly named it for what it was—a "crime," "transgression," or "sin," depending on the translation. Clearly naming and owning the wrong that has been done is the beginning of reconciliation.

Truthfully acknowledging a wrong is generally expected by those whose forgiveness is being sought. It is embedded in more formal practices such as victim-offender mediation, which characteristically begin with both offender and victim sharing the "truth" of what they have experienced.

At the level of nations, truth and reconciliation commissions also characteristically begin with truth speaking. The South African Truth and Reconciliation Commission of the early post-apartheid period of the 1990s, as one example, established truth speaking as one of its cardinal principles: "The Commission was founded in the belief that…one must establish as 'complete a picture as possible' of the injustices committed in the past…."[3]

Reconciliation, to begin with, is then not rooted in forgetting, but in remembering. As the South African Commission notes in its final report, "An inclusive remembering of painful truths about the past is crucial to the creation of national unity and transcending the divisions of the past."[4]

Forgiveness

"Forgive our crime," the brothers pleaded as they approached Joseph. In the Genesis record, this is a breakthrough. This is the first recorded instance in which forgiveness, the second step on the path to reconciliation, is directly asked of another. Thus this is a remarkable, poignant moment.

But is the moment to be discounted, as some have suggested, viewing the brothers as continuing their deceptive ways by putting words into their dead father's mouth when they quoted him as having said: "Say this to Joseph: I ask you to forgive your brothers' crime and wickedness; I know they did you harm." This common interpretation can be traced back to the rabbis of the ancient world, who questioned: "But where did he give such orders? We do not find that he ever gave such orders."[5] This argument from silence – the absence of an independent report of the order to forgive – is overshadowed by other evidence from the text, and thus questionable.

To begin with, Joseph raised no such concern. Rather, we are told, he was "moved to tears" by their words. Yet, admittedly, tears can be ambiguous. Were these tears of resignation that the brothers would never change their lying ways? Or, were they tears over their lack of trust in him? Or, perhaps, were these tears over his father's lack of confidence that he would do right by his brothers after he was gone? Our Genesis storyteller does not clarify.

Interestingly, if truthful, the brothers' report may well express the culmination of Father Jacob's own moral development. In his earlier encounter with his twin brother on the occasion of his homecoming, Jacob had moved as far as conciliation, as I have earlier noted, but fell short of reconciliation. There had been tears then, too. Yet the continuing saga of his life, which he characterized for Pharaoh as "hard" upon his arrival in Egypt, seemed also to be one of continuing growth, as a close reading of the text suggests. Could it be, then, that Jacob, before he died, remembered the fear that he had felt when he returned from exile and could not avoid meeting his estranged brother? And could it be that he foresaw that his death would surface similar fears in his sons? And could it be that he desired that his sons would do better than he had, as parents sometimes desire that their children will move beyond the limits and failings of their own lives?

Such an interpretation, while also speculative, seems more plausible than the guess that the brothers, after all they had been through, were again being deceptive. And if correct, might we then see these last words of Jacob as the summit of his own moral development? And perhaps, even further, suggestive for all his descendants to forgive? And if so, the moral peak toward which the entire book has been ascending?

The Hebrew word *nāśā'*, here translated as "forgiveness," was quite familiar to Jacob. It is a common Hebrew verb. Its literal meaning is to carry, bear, lift up, and the like. Coincidentally, *nāśā'* is also the acronym for the National Aeronautics and Space Administration (NASA) in the United States, which also has to do with lifting things up.

Jacob knew what it meant to bear a heavy load in need of lifting. Earlier he used this word to describe his inner hope prior to meeting his brother Esau upon his return from his uncle Laban. After marshalling his impressive gift of goats, sheep, camels, cattle and donkeys, Jacob had thought: "I may appease him [Esau] with the present that goes ahead of me, and afterwards I shall see his face; perhaps he will accept [*nāśā'*] me" (32:20). In this context *nāśā'* is commonly translated as "accept," consistent with Jacob's dominant motive in that narrative of winning his brother's favor. In the final conversation on the occasion of Jacob's actual meeting with Esau, nevertheless, the word never appears.

In the ending narrative of the brothers' approach to Joseph, unlike their father's earlier encounter with his brother Esau, they brought no gifts to appease other than what might be considered the most important gift they could bring; namely, the gift of confession. This they complemented with the honor of their father's word to forgive—to lift the burden.

Beyond the evidence of Joseph's tears, Joseph also had very practical reasons to believe his brothers were authentic and not deceiving, for he had had the opportunity to test them when earlier they had first arrived in Egypt in search of food. This was no easy forgiveness, or "lift off."

To understand this, we need to return to the earlier story of the brothers' first arrival in Egypt in search of food. There they had met Joseph as second-in-command in the country and responsible for famine relief, but they had not recognized him. He took advantage of this situation to put them through a series of tests.

First, he charged them with being spies. Their denials and his repeated insistence that they were indeed spies evoked some critical family information: "There were twelve of us, my lord, all brothers, sons of one man back in Canaan; the youngest is still with our father, and one is lost." The youngest, of course, was Joseph's only full brother, Benjamin. Both were sons of Jacob by Rachel, his favorite wife, as earlier noted.

Professing doubt about the brothers' truthfulness, Joseph threw the brothers into prison and demanded that they choose one from among them to return home and bring back the younger brother they had mentioned. The others, meanwhile, would be held as hostages. So the truth of their story would be validated.

After three days in prison, Joseph changed his strategy and offered them a deal. It was a hard deal, but better than what he had initially demanded. Instead of holding all but one as hostage, he now changed the formula and offered to release all but one. But they would still have to return with their youngest brother to prove their truthfulness.

The brothers consented to the offer, and then conversed among themselves in their own language, assuming Joseph did not understand, since they had spoken to him through an interpreter. "No doubt," they said to each other, "we are being punished because of our brother. We saw his distress when he pleaded with us and we refused to listen. That is why this distress has come on us." Reuben, the oldest, who had opposed killing Joseph and had been absent when the rest had sold him to the Ishmaelites, then declared to the others: "Did I not warn you not to do wrong to the boy? But you would not listen, and now his blood is on our heads, and we must pay."

Joseph, overhearing this conversation, was moved to tears, which nevertheless he hid from his brothers. Then moving to action, Joseph had Simeon, the second oldest brother, bound as the hostage who would remain. As the second youngest, Joseph's brothers had sold him into slavery. Now the more powerful, Joseph chose the second oldest to hold as hostage in an interesting symmetry of justice. Then their sacks were filled with grain, and secretly topped by the silver they had used to pay for the grain, perhaps to remind them of the silver they had received when they had sold Joseph into slavery. When they first discovered on their way home that their silver had been returned, they exclaimed: "What is this that God has done to us?"

Upon arriving home, the brothers gave Father Jacob a full account of their journey. When Jacob heard that Benjamin, the youngest of his sons, would have to return with them to Egypt, he protested: "You have robbed me of my children. Joseph is lost; Simeon is lost; and now you would take Benjamin." Then in utter despair, he exclaimed: "Everything is against me."

Reuben, the oldest of the sons, sought to soften Father Jacob's opposition to returning to Egypt with Benjamin by offering his own sons as a guarantee of Benjamin's safety: "You may put both my sons to death if I do not bring him back to you. Entrust him to me, and I shall bring him back." But Jacob was adamant and would not budge. He would simply not risk allowing Benjamin to go with the brothers.

As the famine continued and food ran low, Jacob again instructed his sons to return to Egypt. But the sons knew they could not return without Benjamin, and so another round of intense family conversation began. This time Judah, the fourth brother, took the lead. He reminded Father Jacob of the reality they faced. Then Judah offered himself as a guarantee for Benjamin: "I shall go surety for him, and you may hold me responsible. If I do not bring him back and restore him to you, you can blame me for it all my life." Then he impatiently concluded: "If we had not wasted all this time, we could have made the journey twice by now."

Remember, it was Judah who years before put forward the idea of selling Joseph to the Ishmaelite traders. Now, in contrast, Judah offered to guarantee the safety of his youngest brother, Benjamin. Reluctantly Jacob agreed, and the sons returned to Egypt, with double the amount of silver, a variety of conciliatory gifts for Egypt's second-in-command, and youngest brother Benjamin in tow.

In Egypt they were given a grand reception. They were brought into Joseph's very own house for a meal. The brothers, suspicious of what was transpiring, nevertheless responded to Joseph's inquiries as to the welfare of their family, and then introduced their youngest brother, Benjamin. Mysteriously, and to their amazement, their host sat them around the table in the order of their ages. After the meal, their sacks were filled with grain and their silver again secretly returned. In addition, Joseph's very own silver goblet from which he drank was secretly placed in Benjamin's sack.

At dawn the next day, the brothers loaded the sacks onto their donkeys and headed for home. But before they had gone very far, Joseph sent his steward in pursuit of them, accusing them of stealing his very own silver goblet. Protesting, they declared their innocence. A search, nevertheless, surfaced not only the returned silver, but also the goblet in Benjamin's sack. The brothers knew that they were now in deep trouble. Upon their hasty return to the city, they threw themselves on the ground before Joseph, as he berated them for their thievery. It was Judah, then, who stepped forward as the spokesperson for the brothers:

> What can we say, my lord? What can we plead, or how can we clear ourselves? God has uncovered our crime. Here we are, my lord, ready to be made your slaves, we ourselves as well as the one who was found with the goblet.

But Joseph had his own designs. No, he replied, only the one who had the goblet will be held; the rest were free to leave.

Judah, then, moved in closer to Joseph. He spoke movingly on behalf of his father, family and younger brother, Benjamin, reviewing recent events and detailing critical moments in the family's history. He then climaxed his narrative by offering his own life as a substitute for Benjamin:

> Indeed, my lord, it was I who went surety for the boy to my father. I said, "If I do not bring him back to you, then you can blame me for it all my life." Now, my lord, let me remain in place of the boy as my lord's slave, and let him go with his brothers. How can I return to my father without the boy? I could not bear to see the misery which my father would suffer.

Unlike Judah's earlier suggestion to sell Joseph into slavery, he now offered to become a slave in the place of his youngest brother, Benjamin. With this revelation of a transformed Judah, we are told that "Joseph was no longer able to control his feelings," and he proceeded to reveal himself to his brothers.

Returning, then, to the end of the story, note that Joseph previously had been in a position to take his brothers through some rigorous testing. Given the guilt and remorse he had silently overheard in their unguarded conversations, climaxed by Judah's offer to be a substitute for his younger brother, Joseph had reason to believe that his brothers had changed and were authentic in their plea for forgiveness.

Indeed, in the face of this earlier testing, it would have been quite daring for the brothers to not speak truth to Joseph, and uncharacteristic for Joseph to tolerate deception. His ending tears, then, may be better understood as tears of disappointment in their lack of trust in him.

From the standpoint of the brothers, nevertheless, their lack of trust is understandable. For the brothers, as long as Father Jacob was alive, had not really had the opportunity to test Joseph. So, now, with the restraining presence of Father Jacob gone, would the true Joseph be revealed as other than he had appeared? That is the question.

When all those pressures that keep us moving in a particular direction have been stripped away and we stand naked and bare before the world, so to speak, will our true character be revealed as other than the image we have presented? Have we truly forgiven? So the earlier tests in which Joseph tested his brothers were now complemented by the test of his own person. Was Joseph still the arrogant brother of his youth? The tattletale? Would he now tell Pharaoh what his brothers really did to him? And have them all tossed in prison? Would he now dredge up the dreams of his youth and declare to his brothers: I told you so! And demand their submission. We are told that Joseph remembered his earlier dreams when his brothers first appeared in Egypt, as we can imagine he would, but there is no record that he ever said a word about them to his brothers in Egypt, or that he ever used them against his brothers.

Joseph's response to his brothers' plea for forgiveness confirmed that he too passed the test. He, too, had matured. As Alan T. Levenson proposes: "The brat has become a *mentsch*."[6] Indeed, a real *mentsch*, a person of "noble character."

In this narrative, both forgiveness sought and forgiveness granted were tested, validated and confirmed. Forgiveness, linked with restitution where needed and possible, is then a second step toward reconciliation. Forgiveness and restitution both contribute to what has been called "making things right."

Recent interest in forgiveness, as witnessed by the amount of attention it has received, is perhaps akin to its late appearance in Genesis. Religious folks have long talked the language of forgiveness, but today it is a language spoken more broadly. Books and articles on the subject have been written from a variety of perspectives. Research on forgiveness spans a breadth of topics, as illustrated in perhaps the largest initiative to date, "A Campaign for Forgiveness Research" (1999-2005), inaugurated with a multi-million dollar grant from The John Templeton Foundation. Adding prestige to the Campaign were co-chairs Archbishop Desmond Tutu, Ruby Bridges Hall, and Robert Coles, along with former president Jimmy Carter as Campaign Endorser. Forty-six "innovative research projects" were funded during this six-year Campaign.

Yet stories of actual persons who have forgiven those who have harmed them, sometimes even before being asked, have particularly captured the imagination of publics in our time. My beginning story of Gladys Staines in India is only one example.

Repentance, or "future intentions"

Confession and forgiveness were followed by a declaration of future intentions, what in biblical language we might count as evidence of repentance—a change in direction. From here on, Joseph's brothers declared, "we are your slaves."

Repentance, as a third step in reconciliation, is of critical interest to those who have been harmed. Those who have been injured may have heard offenders speak truth and may have even forgiven, yet the question remains, whether implicit or explicitly stated, will they be reinjured? Policy makers, likewise, want to know whether restorative justice processes such as victim-offender mediation programs reduce recidivism; that is, do offenders redirect their lives through these processes, or do they keep offending?

Repentance as in clarifying future intentions is a critical part of a full reconciliation process. To be successful, moreover, community support systems may be needed. As humans we often need support and accountability systems to assure that a change in direction actually happens. Traditional cultures often have established ways to provide this support. Modern industrial societies sometimes have to invent such ways. It stands to reason that placing offenders in the context of healthy support systems to which they are accountable is more likely to achieve positive results than placing them in the context of like others who are more likely to reinforce their harmful behavior.

In the Joseph narrative, future intentions are clarified by both parties to the conflict. The brothers' declaration of submission is countered by Joseph's offer of grace, seeing the larger hand of God in what had transpired in these events:

> "Do not be afraid. Am I in the place of God? You meant to do me harm; but God meant to bring good out of it by preserving the lives of many people, as we see today. Do not be afraid. I shall provide for you and your dependents." Thus he comforted them and set their minds at rest.

Rather than claiming the role of master, Joseph embraced the role of servant, declaring that he would serve his brothers by providing for them and their families. Joseph thus modeled what some today call "servant leadership."

It seems also that Joseph's view of God had grown. He saw God as not only preserving the lives of his immediate family, but also the lives of "many people," which included, of course, the outsider Egyptians. So if all the families of the earth were to be blessed through the descendents of Abraham, as God had earlier promised, the Egyptians were surely among those first blessed.

The story thus ends on two levels. God is able to take the injustices of humans and turn them to good, as the story reveals. Joseph could testify to this goodness as he saw the greater hand of God in what had happened. Injustices, nevertheless, are not thereby excused. The brothers carried a burden for nearly forty years which they knew still needed to be lifted. So they confessed their crime and pleaded for forgiveness. They then committed themselves to a different future as evidence of their repentance. So past, present and future came together in what counts for reconciliation. After nearly forty years, these brothers could finally walk arm-in-arm down the pathway to where peace is at home.

Conclusion

How, then, was it at the beginning? The stories of earth's first families as told in Genesis reveal basic pathways for working with conflict. They remain our pathways even today. We may eliminate those with whom we are in conflict, separate in all of its varieties, conciliate or reconcile.

The book rings with realism. Family struggles can be intense. Though murder is rejected, it keeps happening. Separations, for better or worse, occur. Conciliatory gestures are accepted and rejected. But reconciliations also are realized.

Whereas the post-Eden stories of Genesis begin with the taking of life; they end with the preservation of life. Along the way, these ancient families stumbled toward answers to Cain's foundational moral question, "Am I my brother's keeper?", climaxed in the end with the story of the reconciliation of Joseph and his brothers.

The underlying truth throughout is that we are all created in the image of God and so brothers and sisters in the family of God. As we have learned from Abraham, not only should we not kill each other, but we also should not quarrel. Rather, we should work to find constructive resolutions to the conflicts that inevitably come our way.

In the midst of the struggles of these ancient families, then, there is good news. Pathways beyond murder do exist, including the ultimate pathway of reconciliation. That, indeed, is good news, and so the book might well be retitled, *The Gospel According to Genesis.*

BEST PRACTICE
Restorative Justice

Restorative justice is current language for making things right where harm has occurred in a relationship. "Reconciliation" is longer, historic language for such a process. What restorative justice entails is modeled in this chapter by Joseph and his brothers. Practice today is very similar. In usual practice, it begins with someone taking the initiative. Cultures differ in this regard. But whether one directly involved as victim or offender begins, or perhaps an uncle or aunt, or perhaps an agreed-upon mediator, or brothers as in the case of Joseph and his brothers, someone needs to take the initiative. In formal practice, structured listening often follows until both sides are satisfied that they have been heard. Problem solving then follows, working toward agreement as to what it will take to make things as right as possible.

I once mediated a situation in which a young boy had stolen a purse from an elderly woman. She had lost not only money, but more important to her were some valued pictures that had not been recovered. As we worked toward making things as right as possible, repaying what could be repaid, and had come to an agreement to which the boy's mother had also given her consent, I asked if they yet had anything to say to each other. The boy surprised me when he volunteered, "Yes, I haven't yet asked for forgiveness." Though a young boy, he understood that more was yet needed.

The restorative justice process in which both those harmed and their offenders actively listen to each other, and then make things as right as possible, is a best practice. When climaxed with forgiveness asked and granted, it is even better.

PART II
Jesus: Transformative Pathways

I will lead the blind by a road they do not know,
By paths they have not known I will guide them.
I will turn the darkness before them into light,
the rough places into level ground.
-Isaiah 42:16

Peace is not something you wish *for;*
it's something you make, something you do,
something you are, and something you give away.
-Robert Fulghum, *All I Really Need to Know I Learned in Kindergarten*

Lord, make me an instrument of Thy peace....
-Francesco d'Assisi (1182-1226)

CHAPTER 6
The View From a Galilean Hillside

ANCIENT HEADLINES
(as they might have appeared in today's media)

Bethlehem Infant Proclaimed to be King

Young Student Impresses Temple Rabbis

New Teacher Proclaims Radical Message

Change Required to Fulfill the Law and Prophets According to Galilean Hillside Preacher

TODAY'S HEADLINES
(as they have appeared in today's media)

Bethlehem Christmas joyful, crowded, rainy
AP Worldstream, December 24, 2011

Teachings of Jesus offer radical social alternative
the Irish Times, June 26, 2007

Christians mark somber Good Friday in troubled Jerusalem
AP Worldstream, March 29, 2002

Joy embraces Russians as Easter celebrations get underway
Philippines News Agency, April 24, 2011

"How many biological brothers did Jesus have?" Now and then I have asked this question. I have yet to find anyone who when first asked can give me the correct answer, much less name all his brothers. Yet both New Testament Gospels of Matthew and Mark tell us he had four brothers named James, Joseph, Simon and Judas, and several sisters, not named (Matthew 13:55-56, Mark 6:3). There could well have been as many as nine children in the family of Joseph and Mary, five brothers and four sisters, as happened to be the case in my father's family of birth. And like my carpenter father, carpenter Jesus, too, seems to have lost his father when he was still young, leaving a widowed mother with a nest full of children. Being the oldest son, that also left Jesus with special responsibilities, including dealing with sometimes contentious younger brothers.

Ironically, it is through the skeptics of Jesus's divinity that we learn the names of his brothers. In the Gospel accounts, his fellow villagers name the brothers as evidence that Jesus is just one of them, and hardly Messiah or Divine. The temptation of believers today, however, is to focus on his divinity to the neglect of his humanity. So what difference does it make how many brothers he had? Well, he, too, had to learn how to live with four brothers and several sisters.

As we have seen in the Genesis accounts, family life can be challenging. We can assume that it was no less for Jesus, as it is no less for us. And, as I noted in the Introduction to this work, it is in our families of origin that we first learn to work with conflict. I cited James Gilligan's observation that "all of our basic problem-solving, problem-exacerbating, and problem-creating strategies, for living and dying, are learned first at home."[1] Our Genesis explorations have shown us such strategies as revealed in earth's first families.

I, too, learned strategies for working with conflict and making peace in my family of origin. These strategies were uniquely shaped by my family's membership in a second family of faith. In this sense, we were a blended family of birth and conviction, not unlike the families of Genesis we have explored, and all families of faith.

So, also, it was with Jesus. Jesus was born into a devout Jewish family of faith. His, too, was a blended family of birth and conviction. While we know little of Jesus's childhood and youth, it is hard to imagine that this family unit was not without occasional tensions, as the earlier families of the first Genesis. We do not know whether Joseph and Mary shared the unique story of their marriage with their children when they were still young, complicated as it was by Mary's surprise pre-marriage pregnancy with Jesus. Or, whether Jesus's younger brothers and sisters were aware of his bold claim as a precocious twelve-year old that the Jerusalem temple was his Father's house. Setting one child apart as unique in a family, even if the oldest, is cause for sibling jealousy and rivalry, as we have noted in the Genesis stories. Indeed, we do know that later there were tensions in Jesus's birth family over his public ministry, which led him to make that famous statement about prophets not being without honor "except in their hometown, and among their own kin, and in their own house" (Mark 6:4, Matthew 13:57). But more on this in the next chapter.

When Jesus began his public ministry around the age of thirty, we can assume that he was well versed in the stories of his tradition as passed on by his parents and the likely synagogue school of his home town of Nazareth. Moreover, his life's experiences and observations, not only just in his family, but also in the context of a country occupied by a hated enemy, would have shaped his perspectives. His teachings and modeling occurred in this context.

As a follower of Jesus, as for all of his followers, his life and teachings constitute another genesis, or beginning. So, my question—How was it at this beginning?—I now ask of him.

As with the first Genesis, this second Jesus genesis, too, is acknowledged by all three of the Abrahamic religions of the world, but in different ways. For persons of Jewish faith, Jesus is a great rabbi, or teacher, though not Messiah. For Muslims, he is one of many prophets, son of Mary, but not Son of God. Mohammad, in a Hadith (saying), says: "I am the closest of all people to Jesus, son of Mary, in this world and the Hereafter; for all prophets are brothers, with different mothers but one religion."[2] For Christians, Jesus is Son of God, Savior and Lord.

Warrant for paying attention to the life and teachings of Jesus comes from each of these perspectives. If respected as teacher, surely his teachings should be attended to. Likewise, if regarded as a prophet, surely his prophetic voice should be heard with care. And if Savior and Lord, surely what he commands should be followed with due diligence. Jesus's very own invitation is to all: "He that has ears to hear, let him hear."

The Meaning of Peace Inherited by Jesus

Jesus inherited a tradition. He did not appear in a vacuum. His inheritance was that of the Hebrew Bible, or as Christians call it, the Old Testament. The key word for peace in the Hebrew Bible is *shalom*, meaning to be in a right and just relationship with God, fellow humans and the created order. *Shalom* thus means much more than a mere absence of conflict. Indeed, pursuit of such a just peace may produce conflict with forces that undermine it. So it was with Jesus as he pursued bringing such a peace on earth as in heaven. It is such a *shalom* peace that followers of Jesus are also called to bring on earth—a peace characterized by a right relationship with God, fellow humans and the created order.

Non-Cooperation with Evil – A Foundational "No"

Prior to the beginning of Jesus's public ministry, we are told by the writers of the synoptic gospels of Matthew, Mark and Luke that Jesus spent forty days and nights in the wilderness during which time he fasted. Thereafter, in a weakened and vulnerable state, he was tempted by the devil. As in the first Genesis creation story, evil appeared as a beginning temptation designed to undermine all that might follow.

Jesus's first temptation was addressed to his physical condition; namely, his hunger. But Jesus refused to yield to the devil's suggestion that he turn stones into bread. Neither did he yield to the two subsequent temptations offering him power and wealth. In all, Jesus refused to yield to the devil, unlike Eve and Adam in the first Genesis.

Non-cooperation with evil is foundational to all else in making peace the Jesus way. Such non-cooperation may find expression in our time in such simple matters as not cheating, whether as students in school or as adults in our dealings with each other; not participating in corruption as in bribery and its kin; refusing to engage in dishonest transactions; refusing to obey superiors who would have us lie to gain an advantage for their organization or business; deceiving others by not telling the full truth; stealing by taking what is not ours; participating in unjust actions; and the like. Jesus's response to Satan was a resounding "no." But a "no" also implies a "yes," which then leaves us with the question of what else he had to say.

The Sermon on the Mount

The Hebrew Bible ends with its readers slouching towards Bethlehem, to recall the image of the Irish poet, William Butler Yeats. While the village, first Bethlehem and then Nazareth, was Jesus's first home, his adult journey took him through the wilderness to the mountain. And so it was on a Galilean hillside that Jesus, as a young upstart rabbi, boldly proclaimed that he had come to fulfill the law and the prophets. His sermon—the Sermon on the Mount—has since become the most famous in history.

Jesus's Sermon is his paramount declaration of God's vision for humanity. Much in the Sermon is not new, but a succinct restatement of what God's people had heard in the past. But more than that, the Sermon also challenges accommodations made along the historical journey of ancient Israel, as well as contrary contemporary motivations that are present in every age.

In the early church, "no portion of the Scriptures was more frequently quoted and referred to" by writers than the Sermon on the Mount, Warren S. Kissinger reports in his history of the interpretation of the Sermon. And of the three chapters in Matthew's Gospel that record the Sermon, Kissinger continues, no chapter appears more often in these early writings than the opening fifth chapter.[3]

Beatitudes

Jesus begins his Sermon with "beatitudes," as they have come to be called. These beginning beatitudes capture historic visions of the righteous as expressed by previous Hebrew prophets and poets. Yet restated in the form they appear in Matthew, they gain a cumulative force that has caused people to return to them again and again over the centuries.

Each begins with the word "blessed," "happy" or "congratulations," as the Greek of the New Testament variously has been translated. However, the Greek word so translated, namely *makarioi*, is itself already a translation, as noted by Elias Chacour, Israeli Palestinian church leader familiar with the ancient languages of the region. He observes that the original *ashray* in Aramaic, the language spoken by Jesus, does not have the passive quality of the Greek or subsequent English translations. Rather, *ashray* means "to set yourself on the right way for the right goal; to turn around, repent; to become straight or righteous."[4]

To illustrate, Chacour translates the usual "blessed are those who hunger and thirst for righteousness, for they shall be filled" as "get up, go ahead, do something, move, you who are hungry and thirsty for justice, for you shall be satisfied." Likewise, he translates "blessed are the peacemakers, for they will be called children of God" as "get up, go ahead, do something, move, you peacemakers, for you shall be called children of God."[5] By extension, the same activist meaning then would also apply to the other beatitudes: actively recognizing one's need for God ("poor in spirit"), embracing mourning, practicing meekness, being merciful, pursuing purity of heart, and living righteously, even under the pressure of persecution.

Chacour, thus, sees the Sermon, from its very beginning, as a call to action. What emerges, then, is not a portrait of a passive community, but an action movie of an assertive community in pursuit of the Kingdom of God on earth.

This beginning stream of beatitudes flows to the climax of the great and wonderfully mixed metaphors of "salt" and "light." To actively live out these beatitudes, Jesus states, is to be "salt" and "light" in the world. And when people so live together in community, they are like a city perched on a hill which cannot be hid. A gesture from Jesus would no doubt have called his listeners' attention to such near-by hill-top cities in view from their hillside pews. Then, perhaps borrowing a lamp from a nearby listener, Jesus concludes this opening sequence of the sermon: "Like the lamp, you must shed light among your fellows, so that, when they see the good you do, they may give praise to your Father in heaven" (REB).

Contrary Motives

Following this opening declaration of the righteous, Jesus addresses a series of contrary motives that compromise true righteousness: bounded traditionalism, obsession with approval expressed by applause, preoccupation with wealth, self-justifying judgmentalism and careless treatment of that which is holy. Following his indictment of each contrary motive, he offers a better way, culminating at the end in a cascade of mixed metaphors contrasting narrow and wide gates, good and bad fruit trees, and finally a wise man who built his house on rock that withstood the raging storm, and a foolish man who built his on sand, which fell with "a great crash" when battered by the storm. Indeed, as translated in *The Complete Gospels*, "Its collapse was colossal."

The whole of the sermon may be understood as Jesus's vision for a *shalom* world—a peaceable kingdom of God. Peaceable, however, not merely as the absence of conflict, but the presence of all required to be in a right and just relationship with God, fellow humans and the created order.

For Jesus, the inherited traditions of the law and the prophets fell short of a full realization of such a shalom world. So at this new beginning, he set forth what it would take for the law and the prophets to be fully realized. In the first of the contrary motives of the sermon, he particularly addresses implications for human relationships. It is here that I will focus primary attention, given my larger purpose in this work.

The Contrary Motive of Bounded Traditionalism

Tradition is like a great river fed over the years by many streams; some pollute with the soil of erosion and human waste, while others purify with the pristine water of mountain springs, reminiscent of the river's very own source.

Tradition powerfully shaped the identity of the first century Jewish community, as it continues to shape Jewish, Christian, Islamic and like communities, even today. When identity is wrapped in tradition, members of such communities are particularly resistant to change. Witness the Jewish musical, *Fiddler on the Roof*. The musical opens with its theme song of "Tradition," and the continuing story portrays Father Tevye's struggles and pain as his daughters push beyond what they perceive to be confining boundaries of the tradition.

For Jesus, tradition is not to be rejected, but transformed and purified. For traditions, as I have noted, are easily polluted by the currents of time, sometimes drifting into the retention of forms and legalisms devoid of spirit and deeper meanings.

Jesus was not the first to recognize drift in his tradition. The Hebrew prophets of earlier centuries strongly railed against such drift. Prophetic pronouncements such as Hosea's—"For I desire steadfast love and not sacrifice, the knowledge of God rather than burnt offerings"— vividly illustrate the prophetic voice against drift that has led to the loss of the deeper meanings of the traditional rituals (Hosea 6:6).

Prophets were sometimes joined by poets, who, too, yearned for restoration and a time and place where:

> Steadfast love and faithfulness will meet;
> righteousness and peace [*shalom*] will kiss each other.
> Faithfulness will spring up from the ground,
> And righteousness will look down from the sky
> (Psalm 85:10-11).

A vision of recovery, hence, was not new, but its realization remained a challenge in Jesus's time, as it has continued to be a challenge in every time.

Jesus, then, begins his address of the motivation of tradition by carefully framing his prophetic critique: "Do not think that I have come to abolish the law or the prophets; I have come not to abolish but to fulfill," or "to complete." Thus Jesus positions himself in continuity with his inherited tradition. Fulfillment, or completion, is his operational goal; not denial or rejection. Early church father John Chrysostom confirms: "His sayings were no repeal of the former, but a drawing out, and filling up of them….either by adding what is lacking or by doing what it contains."[6]

This same sense of fulfillment was expressed by Jesus on the occasion of a return visit to his home town of Nazareth after beginning his public ministry. Using the village synagogue as his platform, he declared his mission to be in the tradition of the eighth century BCE prophet Isaiah:

> The Spirit of the Lord is upon me,
> because he has anointed me
> to bring good news to the poor.
> He has sent me to proclaim release to the captives
> and recovery of sight to the blind,

to let the oppressed go free,
to proclaim the year of the Lord's favor.
(Luke 4:18-19; Isaiah 61:1-2).

Jesus's concluding reference to "the year of the Lord's favor" has been understood as a perpetual fulfillment of the Mosaic year of Jubilee—that ending year of every fifty year cycle in which life would be restored to what it had been at the beginning of the cycle.

To fulfill a tradition does not require its rejection. As a wheel is an extension of the foot, to use media scholar Marshall McLuhan's aphorism, so Jesus saw himself as an extension of "the law and the prophets." A wheel does not contradict the foot, as Jesus's teachings do not contradict "the law and the prophets." For Jesus, fulfillment, rather, is to complete what has been begun in an accelerated, cosmic movement towards the ultimate reconciliation of all (Colossians 1:19-20). So is *shalom* (Hebrew), *salaam* (Arabic), *eirene* (Greek), and peace (English), as expressed in all of the languages of earth, to be realized on earth as in heaven.

In the Sermon on the Mount, Jesus follows his statement of purpose with six sayings, which are commonly referred to as "antitheses." This designation follows the common translation of the introductory, formulaic phrase for each of the sayings: "You have heard that it was said…but I say to you…"

The Greek conjunction translated as "but," however, may also be translated as "moreover" or "and." The common "but" translation suggests "opposition to" or "contradiction of" the inherited tradition. "Moreover" and "and" suggest extensions of what precedes. Jesus is not to be limited by any of these possible translations. Rather, he chooses in each of the six sayings to clarify how the past may be fulfilled in the present. In regard to some, "moreover" appears to be the better translation, while in others he appears to be approaching opposition suggested by "but." To force all into the category of "antitheses" is to mislead. Much better simply to refer to his six sayings as Jesus's fulfillment series, following his language in the Sermon itself.

In a final introductory note to Jesus's six fulfillment sayings, we may note that embedded in the six is an implicit progression from family (the first three), to neighbor (the next two), and finally to enemy (the last). Family, neighbor and enemy are deeply rooted in the biblical psyche as inclusive words that serve as shorthand for all human relationships. They are understood in the Jewish tradition in both their literal and metaphorical senses. As metaphors, in particular, they are elastic words that stretch to include all. They also overlap in that family members may become neighbors, and family members and neighbors may also become enemies. They function as types rather than exclusive categories. The address of each forms the heart of Jesus's teaching on conflict and peacemaking. In the chapters that follow, then, we will examine Jesus's understanding of each including core virtues, practices and pathways that in each case lead to where peace is at home.

CHAPTER 7
Transformative Pathways for Families

ANCIENT HEADLINES
(as they might have appeared in today's media)

Rabbi Expands the Meaning of Murder

  Galilean Jesus Urges Reconciliation Between Brothers and Sisters

    Teacher Recommends Radical Action of Plucking out a Lustful Eye

      Local Prophet Takes on Controversial Issue of Divorce

      TODAY'S HEADLINES
      (as they have appeared in today's media)

      Teen Murder Suspect Carried "Backpack Of Hatred"
      St. Joseph News-Press, October 24, 2011

    Ending Hatred Born of Murder Apology Brings Forgiveness
    The Boston Globe, December 4, 1988

Sexual purity important in fulfilling the will of God
Daily Herald (Arlington Heights, IL), August 30, 1997

Marriage and divorce; Reflections Today
Manila Bulletin, August 17, 2001

A fellow member of my church family was not happy with me. Representing a competing interest, I had been a participant in blocking a real estate investment that he wanted to make. Given the tension between us, I consulted with our pastor as to how best to deal with it. I was surprised by his response: "Just let it go. He'll get over it." My pastor knew my protagonist well. His response was obviously based on that knowledge. Even so, was my pastor's counsel on target? Is this what Jesus would have said? I wondered.

Who Is My Family?

The question of who is family is not inconsequential. It is a first question to be asked, for how I answer it determines who I will treat according to family norms. So was I right to think that my fellow church member was my brother, and so should be treated according to what Jesus taught about brothers and sisters?

Who is included and excluded in any of the circles of family, neighbor and enemy, the focus of this and the next two chapters, shapes how I will treat the other. So I begin each of these chapters with the question of who is included in the relevant circle.

The importance of so beginning is highlighted by the noted mythologist Joseph Campbell. Referencing the Hebrew Bible, he observes that "…the ten commandments say, 'Thou shalt not kill.' Then the next chapter says, 'Go into Canaan and kill everybody in it…' The myths of participation and love pertain only to the in-group, and the out-group is totally other. This is the sense of the word 'gentile'—the person is not of the same order."[1]

For Father Tevye, in the musical *Fiddler on the Roof*, not being of the same order is as the difference between a bird and a fish. In his argument with his Jewish daughter Chava over her special relationship with the Russian Fyedka, he finally blurts out: "A bird may love a fish, but where would they make a home together?"

For Sarah in Genesis, exclusion of Hagar and her son from family was justified by labeling Hagar as slave, though she was the second wife of Abraham, and Ishmael, her son, had been born to assure that the inheritance would remain in the family.

Variations abound. In my own childhood, I learned to sing:

> Jesus loves the little children,
> >All the children of the world,
> Red and yellow, black and white
> >All are precious in his sight,
> Jesus loves the little children of the world.

Yet, as I noted in part one of this work, I spent my last years of childhood growing up in a subdivision in a central California town in the post-World War II years which specifically prohibited "any Negro, Japanese, Hindu, Armenian, Malayan, native of the Turkish Empire, Mexican, Chinese, Korean, or any person not of the Caucasian race, or descendant of above named persons" from living in my subdivision neighborhood. While I was gloriously singing in church that Jesus loves all the children of the world, most of the children of the world were excluded from my street. While my family did not create this restriction, when is one complicit by going along with the exclusionary tactics of others when thereby a home for oneself is to be gained?

This human tendency to exclude is not limited to any one group. As mythologist Campbell notes, "brotherhood in most of the myths [stories by which people live] I know of is confined to a bounded community" with "aggression…projected outward."[2]

According to Jesus, then, who is family? That is my first question.

Jesus was born into the earthly family of Mary and Joseph. He was the firstborn, and in Jewish tradition was dedicated to God. As previously noted, he was followed by four brothers—James, Joseph, Simon and Judas—and several sisters, who are not named.

But Jesus also had a two-family identity. He made this two-family identity clear to his parents at the age of twelve in the temple in Jerusalem, noting that he had another Father in whose temple house he happened to be (Luke 2:49). After he began his public ministry around the age of thirty, he made this a public declaration.

As he was teaching one day in a packed house, he was told: "Your mother and your brothers are standing outside, wanting to speak to you." He replied: "Who is my mother, and who are my brothers?" Then "pointing to his disciples, he said, 'Here are my mother and my brothers! For whoever does the will of my Father in heaven is my brother and sister and mother'" (Matthew 12:46-50, Mark 3:31-35; Luke 8:19-21).

Jesus's life, then, was a dance between two families—his birth family and his faith family. His conduct in relation to each was exemplary.

As previously noted, we are told little of Jesus's childhood and youth. It would be interesting to know what his childhood home dynamics were with four brothers and several sisters. We are given a glimpse into parent-child dynamics when at the age of twelve his parents were dismayed upon finding that he was not in the pilgrimage company when returning from the annual Passover celebration in Jerusalem. After finding him back in Jerusalem discoursing with the teachers in the temple, we are told that Jesus returned home and was obedient to his parents, though he had declared that he also had another Father and another house (Luke 2:51).

Subsequent interactions with his birth family reveal a continuing dance—at a wedding feast in Cana (John 2:1-11), attempts by family members to restrain him when people were saying that he had "gone out of his mind" (Mark 3:21), unbelief of his own brothers (John 7:5, Matt. 13:57, Mark 6:4)—and he danced to the end, providing for the continuing care of his mother as the oldest son even as he was dying on the cross (John 19:25-27). Surprisingly, those unbelieving brothers seemed eventually to find their way to faith, so that after his ascension his mother and brothers are identified as being part of the company of the disciples gathered in an upper room in Jerusalem who "were constantly devoting themselves to prayer" (Acts 1:14).

Now, Jesus did have hard things to say about families of birth, declaring that "whoever loves father or mother more than me is not worthy of me; and whoever loves son or daughter more than me is not worthy of me…" (Matt. 10:37). Simultaneously, nevertheless, he strongly condemned those who withdrew support from their parents on the pretext that they were rather directing their support to God, reminding them of the traditional commandment to honor father and mother (Matt. 15:1-9).

Jesus's first core family of faith numbering twelve was a diverse and difficult lot. They were hardly the temple elite. Several were fishermen by trade. One was a tax collector, for whom the Roman occupation was a means to wealth. Another was a resisting zealot, for whom the Roman occupation meant a call to arms. Judas Iscariot, their treasurer, was of doubtful character, and became known for embezzling money from their treasury (John 12:6). Never expelled from the group, in the end he betrayed Jesus.

Fishermen Peter, James and John emerged as a smaller leadership group among the twelve, though different in nature. James and John were brothers, known for their fiery personalities. Jesus called them *Boanerges,* meaning "Sons of Thunder" (Mark 3:17). And Peter, their emerging leader, could be aggressive on one day and cowardly on the next.

Together these twelve constituted a challenging family struggling toward faith—often slow in understanding and sometimes distracted by internal competition among themselves. Rejecting the easy path of creating a new family of faith out of like-minded persons, Jesus chose to create this new family out of quite diverse persons with different personalities, different vocational backgrounds, different abilities, and the like. And he loved them all, telling them toward the end that they should love each other as he had modeled love toward them (John 15:12).

Until the very end of his life on earth, then, Jesus never forgot either of his families. He modeled a dance between his family of birth and his family of faith, calling his followers to faithfulness in regard to both.

Jesus's expanded notion of his faith family, however, quickly ran into the ruling boundaries of gender (women), illness (leprosy), vocation (tax collectors, prostitutes), race/ethnicity (Samaritans) and outsiders (Gentiles). The wall erected on the boundary between Jew and Gentile was particularly impenetrable. Even though Jesus had declared that all who do the will of God were members of his family, this seed he planted did not fully mature until after he had left this earth.

Simon Peter, foremost among the twelve apostles, was among the first to be confronted with the division in Jesus's family of faith caused by this divide between Jew and Gentile. His rethinking of this formidable barrier began while a guest in the house of another also named Simon, but a tanner by trade, who lived in the Mediterranean coastal town of Joppa, today part of the modern city of Tel Aviv.

One day, as noon approached, Peter went to the top of host Simon's flat-roofed house to pray and wait for his lunch, being hungry. While waiting, we are told he fell into a trance in which he saw something like a large sheet or vessel being lowered from the sky filled with all kinds of animals, reptiles and birds, which as a faithful Jew he considered to be unclean. Peter then heard a voice saying, "Get up, Peter; kill and eat." Objecting, Peter responded: "By no means, Lord; for I have never eaten anything that is profane or unclean." The voice responded: "What God has made clean, you must not call profane." We are told that this happened three times, at which point the sheet was withdrawn into heaven, leaving a puzzled Simon Peter behind.

Peter's vision posed a dilemma. How does one tell the difference between a temptation and a revelation? After all, the choice of what to eat had been clearly established in the tradition for centuries, and had been personally embraced by Peter as a faithful follower of God.

Context may be a partial answer to the question, for at that moment representatives of a Gentile, Roman military officer—a Centurion by rank—appeared at the door of his host's house, and Peter began to make a connection. He was invited to the Centurion's home to the north in the Roman political and military center of Caesarea. The Centurion had had his own vision, also being a religious person. There it was, in the Gentile Centurion's house, that Peter bore witness that "God has shown me that I should not call anyone profane or unclean;" indeed, I now "truly understand that God shows no partiality, but in every nation anyone who fears him and does what is right is acceptable to him" (Acts 10:28, 34-35). Then the Holy Spirit fell upon those present, confirming that all who follow God truly are part of his convictional faith family, whether Jew or Gentile (Acts 10:44).

In brief, then, family for Jesus meant both his family of birth and the larger family of God. This larger faith family transcends all other boundaries, whether racial, tribal, ethnic, national, or otherwise. The Apostle Paul, the first century Jewish Christian missionary to the Gentiles, later stated it succinctly: "There is no longer Jew or Greek, there is no longer slave or free, there is no longer male and female; for all of you are one in Christ Jesus" (Galatians 3:28).

Jesus's Ethic for the Family

The core of Jesus's ethical teachings for the three circles of family, neighbor and enemy is found in the segment of his Sermon on the Mount which I have called his "fulfillment series" (Matthew 5:17-48). This segment, by way of reminder, consists of a series of six teachings. The first three of the six focus on the family (5:21-32).

Murder in the Family (the First in the Series)

Jesus begins, as does the post-Eden portion of Genesis, by addressing the taking of life. As previously noted, the prohibition of murder, with its concomitant provision to be the keeper of brothers and sisters, is where moral development begins.

So it was also affirmed in the Decalogue (ten commandments) of the later Mosaic law. While the first five of the ten commandments speak of honoring God and parents, the sixth is the first in a series of prohibitions against murder, adultery, stealing, lying, and coveting. Murder heads the list.

So it is that Jesus, too, begins at this point. "The first law which Jesus commends to his disciples is the one which forbids murder and entrusts their brother's welfare to their keeping," as German theologian Dietrich Bonhoeffer observes.[3]

Having restated the tradition's rejection of murder, Jesus does not contradict it. Rather, he augments its meaning:

> You have heard that it was said to those of ancient times, "You shall not murder"; and "whoever murders shall be liable to judgment." But [moreover] I say to you that if you are angry with a brother or sister, you will be liable to judgment; and if you insult a brother or sister, you will be liable to the council; and if you say, "You fool," you will be liable to the hell of fire.

Following this lead, Jesus's disciple John put it starkly: "All who hate a brother or sister are murderers..." (1 John 3:15). Though "we must not be like Cain," as John declares, we must also not murder with hate. Love is to be the hallmark of life in the family.

Jesus, however, does not stop with the foregoing. Being a realist, he proceeds in his sermon to offer strategies for dealing with conflicts that inevitably arise in families. He counsels:

> So when you are offering your gift at the altar, if you remember that your brother or sister has something against you, leave your gift there before the altar and go; first be reconciled to your brother or sister, and then come and offer your gift.
>
> Come to terms quickly with your accuser while you are on the way to court with him, or your accuser may hand you over to the judge, and the judge to the guard, and you will be thrown into prison. Truly I tell you, you will never get out until you have paid the last penny.

In the foregoing cases, Jesus places responsibility for initiative on the perceived offender. So, "…if you remember that your brother or sister has something against you, leave your gift there before the altar and go…" Or, if you are accused of wrongdoing and are being taken to court, move quickly to negotiate a settlement.

On the other hand, in a later teaching Jesus places similar responsibility for initiative on victims and observers of wrongdoing: "If your brother does wrong [including against you], go and take the matter up with him…" (Matthew 18:15 REB).

For Jesus, it makes no difference whether you are aware that someone sees you as the wrongdoer, or you see the other as the wrongdoer. In either case, Jesus says "go" and make peace.

Often the most difficult step in peacemaking is that first step of going. So Jesus's beginning word to those who would be peacemakers is perceptive. Simply "go."

Jesus, however, also cautions those who see failures in others not to fall into the trap of what I have called judgmentalism. Later in the Sermon on the Mount, Jesus speaks of the human inclination to see "specks" in another's eye while having a "log" in one's own. "You hypocrite," he says, "first take the log out of your own eye, and then you will see clearly to take the speck out of your neighbor's eye" (Matthew 7:1-5).

But even if one goes with clear vision, one should be prepared to meet resistance. It is therefore useful to go with a plan in mind. The plan Jesus proposed may be called a "stepwise" plan, following conflict theorist Paul Wehr's description of a similar approach used by Mahatma Gandhi.[4] Jesus's plan begins with a one-on-one personal, face-saving approach. That is the first step. If the matter is not resolved at this level, a second step follows. Take one or two others with you following the Mosaic Law's provision that "only on the evidence of two or three witnesses shall a charge be sustained" (Deuteronomy 19:15). If still not resolved, a third step is to take it to the *ekklesia*, variously translated as church, congregation, synagogue, assembly or community, for final discernment (Matthew 18:15-17).

Jesus affirms the authority and power of the community in his elaboration of this third step: "Truly I tell you, whatever you bind on earth [prohibit] will be bound in heaven, and whatever you loose on earth [permit] will be loosed in heaven" (Matthew 18:18).

Embedded in this simple, three-step process, then, are potential complexities that the plan accommodates. So, if the perceived offender ("sinner"), when first approached, gives attention and agrees that a wrong has been committed and seeks to make it right, the matter may be resolved at this first step without the complicating dynamics of saving face when others are immediately drawn into the picture.

Not listening, however, may be understood not only as refusing to give attention, but also as not agreeing. For example, the perceived offender may dispute the facts set forth by the visitor, or disagree that the matter of concern is in fact wrong. In either case, the second step involving one or two others provides an enlarged context for reviewing the matter.

If disputes regarding facts or the rightness or wrongness of the matter continue, the case is moved on to the community (*ekklesia*). The community is the final court for discerning facts or whether the behavior of concern is "bound" (not permitted) or "loose" (permitted).

In the end, should the matter of concern be considered "bound" by the *ekklesia*, the facts of an assumed violation established by multiple witnesses, and the offender still resistant, only then is the now confirmed offender to be viewed as an *ethnikos*, translated variously as "heathen," "Gentile" and "pagan," or as a tax collector of the time.

Jesus, however, did not cut himself off from those so separated and in continuing need of redemption. He was known to welcome, and even eat with sinners. He told stories about going in search of those lost as one would when a sheep or coin is lost. He even told a story which suggested that at times one might have to patiently wait for sinners to come to their senses. A son, as the story goes, demanded his inheritance before his father had died, and then proceeded to squander it. Eventually reduced to poverty and desperate, he returned to his father, who had been waiting for him to come back, and now embraced him and welcomed him home. As this story suggests, if in the end a faith family discerns a matter to be "bound" and an offender remains unrepentant, separations need not end relationships. The motive of wishing that none should be lost calls for continuing relationships of respect and care, which simultaneously may require the patience of the waiting father as portrayed in this story of the prodigal son.

On the other hand, if the matter of concern surprisingly is considered to be "loose" by the *ekklesia*, the resisting person may in fact have helped the community to discern a greater truth and change its norms. This potential for change is illustrated by a complementary story of shepherds and sheep told by Nelson Mandela of South Africa. Mandela attributes his understanding of leadership to a story of sheep and shepherds told by a regional African chief in whose household he grew up after his father died. This leader observed that shepherds walk and so lead from behind the flock, "letting the most nimble go out ahead, whereupon the others follow, not realizing that all along they are being directed from behind."[5]

So it was also in the New Testament church. Paul and Barnabas were among those "more nimble," who spread the good news of Jesus to the Gentiles without imposing all of the restrictions of their sending community, among them the very old and firmly entrenched tradition since Abraham of circumcision. On the other hand, some early Jewish Christians invoked the tradition insisting that Gentile Christians must be circumcised. When there was "fierce dissension" over the issue in the Gentile city of Antioch at the first levels of Jesus's stepwise process, the matter was escalated to the mother church in Jerusalem to determine whether the matter was "bound" or "loose" (Acts 15). In a radical departure from Jewish tradition and practice, the Jerusalem church declared the matter to be "loose" for Gentile Christians.

They further reported this resolution as a consensus between themselves and the Holy Spirit (Acts 15:28). In Jesus's earlier conclusion to his stepwise proposal, he had similarly noted: "For where two or three are gathered in my name, I am there among them" (Matthew 18:20). Speaking out of the tradition, other ancient rabbis likewise affirmed: "But when two sit together and words of Torah pass between them, the Divine Presence [*Shekinah*] rests between them…"[6]

The change, then, that results from the stepwise process of Jesus may be surprisingly different from what was first expected. "Nimble sheep," who at first may be viewed as sinners, may in fact lead to a change in the community itself, even in the case of long, entrenched traditions such as circumcision.

Jesus's stepwise proposal raised yet another question for Peter, leading student-disciple of Jesus: "Lord, how often am I to forgive my brother if he goes on wronging me? As many as seven times?" (Matthew 18:21 REB). Peter does not question whether one should forgive a brother or sister who confesses a wrong and seeks to make things right. Jesus had already been clear about that, if in fact Peter had not already understood this from the tradition. Indeed, Jesus had taught that the forgiveness of God was contingent upon a person's willingness to forgive another. In the Sermon on the Mount, Jesus had taught his hillside listeners to pray: "And forgive us our debts, as we also have forgiven our debtors." Jesus had further reinforced the prayer with a commentary: "For if you forgive others their trespasses, your heavenly Father will also forgive you; but if you do not forgive others, neither will your Father forgive your trespasses" (Matthew 6:12, 14-15).

These words reflect a deep identification of God with the created order. So it has been from the very beginning. The violation of another, as in Cain's first violation of his brother, is also a violation of the rule of God, even as in modern criminology a crime is viewed as not only a violation of another, but also an offense against the state.

Modern criminology, however, is deeply flawed in its view that one's debt has been paid when the state's sentence has been fulfilled, even though the matter has not been made right with the actual person harmed. Not so with Jesus. Simply confessing one's sins to God without righting wrongs committed against brothers or sisters is not sufficient. A core point of Jesus's stepwise process of escalation is to encourage persons to make things right with those they have actually harmed on matters confirmed to be wrong.

Furthermore, while God deeply identifies with those wronged, so God also deeply identifies with the confessing sinner. So, "…if you do not forgive others, neither will your Father forgive your trespasses." Old Testament scholar Walter Brueggemann confirms: "Biblical faith offers no God who is not embedded in the fabric of human transactions. Thus estranged brotherliness leads to estrangement from God. Reconciled brotherliness, moreover, leads to reconciliation with God"[7]

Peter, nevertheless, pushes the point: "Lord, how often am I to forgive my brother if he goes on wronging me?" Then Peter added, apparently thinking he was being generous: "As many as seven times?" Jesus replied, "I do not say seven times but seventy times seven" (Matthew 18:21-22 REB). Jesus echoes Lamech from the first Genesis, who would best Cain by avenging himself "seventy times seven." Using the same Hebrew formula for unlimited this or that, Jesus now changes the focus from vengeance to forgiveness. Again Jesus explodes the boundary, not in support of vengeance, but in support of forgiveness.

In brief, then, in this first of Jesus's six sayings in his fulfillment series, expanded by related teachings, he moves brothers and sisters beyond murder to reconciliation and restoration to community. So "go", Jesus says, with vision unobstructed by logs in one's own eyes, whether offender, victim or observer of wrong-doing, and make peace. Escalate in a controlled, stepwise manner, marshalling nonviolent social power when resistance is encountered, while remaining humble and open to the possibility that a perceived sinner may be advancing a greater truth yet to be discerned. Use the power of separation with sensitivity, and allow time for reconciliation. And keep forgiving, even when repetitive requests test your patience. Though you may stumble along the way, keep dancing toward peace in the embrace of whatever your family, including faith family, arrangement may be.

Adultery in the Family (the Second in the Series)

While Jesus focuses on brother and sister relationships in the first of the six sayings, in the second and third he focuses on marital relationships. Here he begins with adultery.

In the patriarchal culture of the first Genesis, adultery does not appear as a major issue. Rather, issues of sibling rivalry and inheritance typically dominate the Genesis family stories, as we have seen. In the subsequent history of Israel, nevertheless, adultery surfaced as a serious issue. Even as noble a king as David in Israel's history was guilty, not only of adultery itself, but also its offspring of manipulated cover-ups and murder. The mix of adultery and power can be deadly. So perhaps it was no accident that when a rich ruler came to Jesus one day asking what he needed to do to inherit eternal life, Jesus cited the historic Decalogue, the second half of which begins with the prohibition of murder and adultery. Surprisingly, however, for this rich ruler, Jesus reversed the order of these two, suggesting perhaps that for rich rulers adultery is the first temptation followed by murder, as had been true in the historic case of King David (Luke 18:18-25).

In the ten commandments of the Mosaic Law, nevertheless, the prohibition of adultery follows on the heels of murder. It also takes second place in Jesus's fulfillment series. Again, while reiterating the tradition, Jesus does not contradict it; rather, he extends it by enlarging its meaning.

> You have heard that it was said, "You shall not commit adultery." But [moreover] I say to you that everyone who

looks at a woman with lust has already committed adultery with her in his heart. If your right eye causes you to sin, tear it out and throw it away; it is better for you to lose one of your members than for your whole body to be thrown into hell. And if your right hand causes you to sin, cut it off and throw it away; it is better for you to lose one of your members than for your whole body to go into hell (5:27-30).

In today's sensual cultures, exacerbated by internet pornography, Jesus's radicalization of adultery to include looking at a woman "with lust" represents a major challenge. It is a significant cause of spousal conflict and distress. Jesus's drastic measures of plucking out eyes and cutting off hands to curb adultery, metaphorical though they be intended, nevertheless indicate the seriousness with which he viewed the problem. Radical surgery is called for.

Adultery follows murder as a major destroyer of family peace. Implicit in Jesus's radicalization of adultery is a vision of purity that challenges the misplaced sensuality of any time, and perhaps most radically, our time. The family dance is compromised when one's vision is impure and distracted.

Divorce in the Family (the Third in the Series)

In his culminating focus on family relationships, Jesus addressed the difficult issue of divorce. The question of justifiable grounds for divorce, of course, was not new. In Part 1 of this work we saw Abraham's struggle over his second wife Hagar as he was caught between Sumerian family law of his native Ur and his first wife's insistence that Hagar and her son Ishmael be separated from the family. For the first century Jewish community in which Jesus lived, it was the Mosaic Law that governed, with its already long history of varied interpretations. So what did Jesus have to say? Again he began with the tradition:

It was also said, "Whoever divorces his wife, let him give her a certificate of divorce." But I say to you that anyone who divorces his wife, except on the ground of unchastity, causes her to commit adultery [or, "makes her the victim of adultery" (Miller)]; and whoever marries a divorced woman commits adultery (5:31-32).

Jesus's teaching on divorce in this and other passages has been much debated by scholars both ancient and modern. These debates often center on disagreements over the grounds for divorce. Different schools of thought existed in Jesus's time, as they exist also today. This was apparent in a later exchange between Jesus and the Pharisees who came to him with the question, "Is it lawful for a man to divorce his wife for any cause?" (Matthew 19:3).

The case for "any cause" could be made by quoting the Torah (e.g. Deuteronomy 24:1-4), which states that a husband might give his wife a certificate of divorce if "he finds something objectionable about her." The wife in this patriarchal culture, of course, had no such right if she found something "objectionable" about him. Had the question, nevertheless, been raised in today's context, it would have cut both ways. Might husband or wife divorce simply because they find "something objectionable" or "obnoxious," to use another translation, in the other? How easy should divorce be?

In rabbinic tradition, divorce "for any cause" has been the view identified with the Rabbi Hillel school of thought. The Rabbi Shammai school limited divorce to adultery, which is the view espoused by Jesus.

In response to the Pharisees' question about divorce for any cause, however, Jesus moved beyond what has been called "boundary thinking" to "centered thinking." He responded by asking the moral question I have focused as central to this work: How was it at the beginning? He said to them:

> Have you not read that the one who made them at the beginning "made them male and female," and said, "For this reason a man shall leave his father and mother and be joined to his wife, and the two shall become one flesh"? So they are no longer two, but one flesh. Therefore what God has joined together, let no one separate (Matthew 19:4-6, cf Genesis 2:20-25).

His Pharisee interrogators, not satisfied, countered with a follow-up question: "Why then did Moses command us to give a certificate of dismissal and to divorce her?" Jesus replied: "It was because you were so hardhearted that Moses allowed you to divorce your wives, but from the beginning it was not so. And I say to you, whoever divorces his wife, except for unchastity, and marries another commits adultery" (Matthew 19:7-9).

The Pharisees might well have bolstered the case for easy divorce by adding the further example of their own beginning as a Jewish people before even Moses. Had God not told Abraham, their historic father, to proceed and dismiss his second wife Hagar and her son as demanded by his first wife Sarah? What might Jesus have said about that?

But in Jesus's moral reasoning, even Abraham is trumped by how it was at the very beginning of the institution of marriage and family as recorded in the creation narratives of Genesis. And while biblical scholars, religious leaders and laity alike may debate justifiable grounds for divorce, as did the rabbis of old, the original moral vision for marriage and family, nevertheless, remains constant.

Weddings continue to celebrate that original vision. Marriage vows that are climaxed with the biblical saying, "What God has joined together, let no one separate," reaffirm that original vision. The subsequent messiness of many marriages in no way diminishes God's vision for holistic and peaceful families. It is that core vision which Jesus lifted up in response to his Pharisee interrogators.

When this vision is not realized and family life does go badly awry, as indeed happens, husbands and wives may well remember Jesus's prohibition against that first pathway of murder, as earlier also prohibited in Genesis and the Mosaic Law. This first prohibition is not insignificant when in the United States, as one example, nearly one in three women murdered each year are murdered by their spouses or boyfriends. And if separations seem to be wise, husbands and wives may well remember that as in the family of Abraham, separations come in many varieties—negotiated, running away, forced and simply moving on as in "lumping it." Separations, moreover, need not end relationships, as Abraham in the first Genesis modeled continuing care for his nephew-brother Lot after they separated. Care for each other and the children of a marriage may continue, even if in new arrangements. Though it may take time, as in Jesus's story of the prodigal son along with the earlier Genesis stories of Jacob and Esau and Joseph and his brothers, conciliation and reconciliation also remain potential pathways to a still better future.

Then there is also grace. One day Jesus broke both cultural and gender norms by speaking alone at a communal well to an outsider Samaritan woman who had had five husbands and was apparently living with a sixth to whom she was not married (John 4:1-42). Had each of her previous five husbands found something "objectionable" or "obnoxious" in her and issued a certificate of divorce? Or, as Hagar in Genesis, had she perhaps fled abuse from her previous husbands? Or, perhaps, had they in succession all died? We do not know, for Jesus's conversation with the woman did not turn into an inquisition about her marital history, but rather into a theological inquiry about the nature of true worship. And because the woman was not quiet about her encounter with Jesus, we are told that "many Samaritans from that city believed in him because of the woman's testimony." All happened because of a woman who had had five husbands and a sixth live-in whom Jesus did not condemn, but took the time to engage in conversation about the nature of true worship.

Jesus's capacity for grace was tested one day when a woman caught in adultery was forcibly ushered into his presence (John 8:3-11). Again he was interrogated by scribes and Pharisees. They reminded him that the Mosaic Law commanded that a woman so caught should be stoned. "Now what do you say?" they asked.

Along with the Shammai school of thought, Jesus had taught that adultery breaks the bond of marriage. So what would he now say? Rather than speaking, we are told that "Jesus bent down and wrote with his finger on the ground." This curious response of seeming avoidance of the question is not accompanied by a report as to what he wrote. So, was he simply buying time to form a response? When the questioners persisted, he stood up and said to them: "Let anyone among you who is without sin be the first to throw a stone at her." And then bending over, he continued to write on the ground. One-by-one, we are told, the woman's accusers quietly faded away, leaving him alone with the woman. Again straightening up, he noted that all had left. Turning to the woman he asked: "Woman, where are they? Has no one condemned you?" Politely she responded: "No one, sir." And then Jesus said: "Neither do I condemn you. Go your way, and from now on do not sin again."

Jesus's extension of grace to the woman was not an endorsement of her behavior; rather, it was an affirmation of his larger mission, not to condemn the world, but to save the world (John 3:17). For Jesus, adultery constituted a boundary that if crossed broke the bonds of marriage. Yet prevailing was his centered understanding of God's original intention for marriage along with his larger redemptive and restorative mission on earth.

Conclusion

In review, then, the first three of the six sayings in Jesus's fulfillment series of his Sermon focus on the family. As in Genesis, so also now with Jesus. The family is our first school in conflict and peacemaking.

While acknowledging the forces of hatred, murder, lust, adultery, and divorce, Jesus set forth alternative pathways that lead to healthy and holistic families, whether literal or metaphorical as in families of faith. Though one may stumble and be in need of grace, Jesus beckons persons of all times and places to dance in rhythmic unity along these pathways which lead to where peace is at home.

BEST PRACTICE
"Go"

In promoting a restored world order in his Sermon on the Mount, Jesus begins with the family, as the Hebrew Bible also begins in Genesis. Murder, adultery and divorce, major disruptors of family life in his time as now, are the focus of his beginning address. He has a word for each. When caught in the web of family conflict, often the most difficult first step is opening a conversation with a brother or sister, husband or wife, child or parent. Risk is involved. And fear can immobilize us. But we can also be surprised. And it is even possible that our going may result in our own transformation as we discover that the other may be more right than we are. Until we go, we do not know. Once having gone, best practices as modeled in part one of this work become options. And then there is what we learn further from Jesus. His stepwise model of escalation when met with resistance, for example, has been replicated in nonviolent versions in our own time by leaders such as Mohandas K. Gandhi of India. And Jesus's strong teaching on forgiveness is no less relevant in our time than it was for Joseph and his brothers in the culminating story of Genesis, and the followers of Jesus in their time. As Jesus sought to fulfill the "law and prophets" of his inheritance, today we are called to fulfill our Jesus inheritance whether we view him as rabbi-teacher, prophet, or Lord and Savior.

CHAPTER 8
Transformative Pathways for Neighbors

ANCIENT HEADLINES
(as they might have appeared in today's media)

Lawyer's Question – Who is my Neighbor? – Inspires Story

Teacher from Nazareth Proclaims the Virtue of Truthful Speech

Radical Rabbi Challenges Historic Teaching of "An Eye for an Eye and a Tooth for a Tooth"

Giving More Than is Demanded is Captured by Itinerant Preacher in Images of Going a Second Mile or Giving Up All of One's Clothes

TODAY'S HEADLINES
(as they have appeared in today's media)

Who is your neighbor?
Haiti Observateur, December 19, 2007

Love even that neighbor?
The Christian Science Monitor, November 12, 2009

Truth, the biggest casualty
The Daily Mirror (Colombo, Sri Lanka), December 28, 2009

Restorative Justice Offers Healing, Great Promise (Editorial)
The Capital Times, December 24, 2003

My mountain neighbor, a lawyer by profession, was very angry with me. In my annual cleanup of dead wood, pine needles and the like surrounding a mountain retreat facility that I managed and maintained, he accused me of trespassing on his adjacent though undeveloped and unoccupied property. In particular, he charged, I had burned a short log he had set aside among other dead wood with the intent to later shape it into a bench as a gift for his wife. Given the distance between corner markers in this mountainous terrain, it was impossible to discern at all points precisely where the boundary ran. His burned log apparently had been somewhere in the vicinity of the boundary. From his perspective, nevertheless, I had committed an injustice. From my perspective, his unmarked log looked no different than other dead wood on the ground, and I had no prior knowledge of his intention. We both had our personal truths, not to speak of the truth of where the boundary actually ran at the point in question. On whose side actually was the log?

Truth and justice are essential ingredients of neighborly relationships. It should be no surprise, then, that truth and justice are also themes of Jesus in his Sermon. Again, however, we first begin with the question of who is in the circle of neighbor.

Who is My Neighbor?

Neighbors, present from the beginning in the family stories of Genesis, figure significantly in the remaining books of the Torah. Indeed, the Mosaic Law came to be summarized in two grand statements: the first focusing on love for God —"Hear, O Israel: The Lord our God is one Lord; and you shall love the Lord your God with all your heart, and with all your soul, and with all your might" (Deuteronomy 6:4-5), and the second on love for neighbor—"you shall love your neighbor as yourself" (Leviticus 19:18).

In this age of immigrants, it is useful to note that the definition of neighbor in the Mosaic Law includes the stranger and the alien in the land. The ancient Hebrews themselves had once been strangers and aliens in Egypt, and they were instructed never to forget this. They were specifically told to also "love the alien as yourself" (Leviticus 19:33-34).

Jesus's further view of the neighbor is best understood through a story. A lawyer came to Jesus one day with a test question: "Teacher, what must I do to inherit eternal life?" Jesus responded with a counter question: "What is written in the law? What do you read there?"

The lawyer responded by quoting that grand summary of the law: "You shall love the Lord your God with all your heart, and with all your soul, and with all your strength, and with all your mind; and your neighbor as yourself." Jesus replied: "You have given the right answer; do this, and you will live."

Then came the inevitable boundary question: "And who is my neighbor?" Jesus responded with a story. A Jewish brother traveling along the well known and dangerous path from Jerusalem to Jericho was robbed, stripped, beaten and left half dead. A priest, a spiritual leader of his in-group, came along, saw him lying by the road side, and passed by on the other side. Likewise a Levite, also a leader among his own, passed by. But then came a Samaritan, an outsider. This outsider of a different ethnic and religious orientation, at risk of being robbed himself, nevertheless stopped and provided first aid, then ambulanced him on his animal to a local inn, and paid the innkeeper to provide further care.

Upon completing the story, Jesus asked: "Which of these three, do you think, was a neighbor to the man who fell into the hands of the robbers?" The answer, of course, was obvious, so he truthfully replied, "The one who showed him mercy." And Jesus said to him, "Go and do likewise" (Luke 10:25-37).

One can imagine that it must have been difficult for the lawyer to acknowledge an outsider, not only as the hero of the story, but also as capable of teaching an insider anything of value. The lawyer seems incapable in his response even to utter the word, "Samaritan."

The story, then, is a two-edged sword. The Samaritan is both hero and teacher, demonstrating what it means to be a neighbor. While the professionally trained insider priest and Levite passed by without practicing that most elementary teaching of their tradition—namely, being their brother's keeper—the outsider Samaritan modeled compassion—binding up wounds, providing ambulance service to the nearest inn, and even paying for further care. In so doing, he extended the ancient principle of being a brother's keeper to even an outsider neighbor.

So again Jesus pushed back the boundary. Not only Samaritans, of course, but the varied outsider groups of his time were drawn into his community, including such fringe groups as prostitutes, tax collectors, lepers and the like.

Jesus's Ethic for Neighbors

In the Decalogue of the Mosaic Law, the ninth and tenth commandments state: "You shall not bear false witness against your neighbor. You shall not covet your neighbor's house; you shall not covet your neighbor's wife, or male or female slave, or ox, or donkey, or anything that belongs to your neighbor" (Exodus 20:16-17). So will *shalom,* or peace, be preserved in the neighborhood.

In the Sermon on the Mount Jesus frames ethical behaviors toward neighbors around the two great themes of speaking truth and doing justice, both implied in the ninth and tenth commandments of the Decalogue of the tradition. In speaking truth and doing justice, then, "the law and the prophets" are further fulfilled.

Pragmatically, speaking truth and doing justice lead to healthy neighborhoods and communities. Without truth and justice, social, political, legal and economic systems are weakened, and become vulnerable to collapse. Anyone minimally observant of our contemporary social, political and economic systems should understand that where lying, cheating and an assortment of injustices exist, the viability of our varied systems is undermined.

As humans, nevertheless, perhaps we should be encouraged inasmuch as the claim has been made that the universe is on the side of truth and justice. The Greek philosopher Aristotle, among early proponents of such a claim, observes that "truth and justice are by nature more powerful than their opposites." "With the right on their side," therefore, humans "have only themselves to thank for the outcome" when wrong wins out over right.[1]

Even in the best of societies, nevertheless, humans succumb to telling less than the truth and to doing less than justice, often in pursuit of some perceived gain. The subsequent weakening of community adds to the significance of the teaching of Jesus.

Speaking Truth (the Fourth in the Fulfillment series)

As Jesus enters the arena of truth speaking, he dramatically throws away the crutch of swearing:

> Again, you have heard that it was said to those of ancient times, "You shall not swear falsely, but carry out the vows you have made to the Lord." But I say to you, Do not swear at all, either by heaven, for it is the throne of God, or by the earth, for it is his footstool, or by Jerusalem, for it is the city of the great King. And do not swear by your head, for you cannot make one hair white or black. Let your word be "Yes, Yes" or "No, No"; anything more than this comes from the evil one (Matthew 5:33-37).

Truth speaking is so elevated by Jesus that the historical crutch of swearing to assure its presence should be irrelevant and not needed. Vows, contracts, covenants, promises and the like should not require swearing to uphold. "Let your word be 'Yes, Yes' or "No, No'; anything more than this comes from the evil one." Strong words, though simple they be.

Swearing is rooted in suspicion. When I was a child, suspicion was countered by the formulaic saying: "Cross my heart and hope to die." In court, adults place one hand on a sacred text while lifting the other and swearing to "speak the truth and nothing but the truth, so help me God." But all of this, Jesus proclaims, should be unnecessary. We are called to live above suspicion. "Yes" should mean "yes" and "no" should mean "no", consistently and always. No help from crutches needed.

Consistent truth speaking, furthermore, is a prerequisite for trust. And trust is essential to establish community. Lie about your neighbor, to begin with, and the destruction of community follows. The ninth of the ten commandments—"You shall not bear false witness against your neighbor"—is therefore of great significance. The New Testament affirms this prohibition, but reframes it in the positive, admonishing us to "speak the truth to our neighbors…" (Ephesians 4:25). But this is only the beginning. All relationships—informal, contractural or otherwise—should be grounded in truth speaking.

Lying, ironically, produces its own judgment. Rabbi Simeon of old confirms: "The punishment of the liar is that even when he tells the truth he is not believed…"[2] Such a consequence is particularly severe when leaders lie, for their lies, like stones thrown into a quiet lake, ripple through larger social, political, economic and other like systems with destructive effects.

Truth, furthermore, should be expressed in love, and not in anger, hatred, vengeance, glee and the like. While Jesus does not make this link in his Sermon, "speaking the truth in love" became a truism of the Apostle Paul (e.g. Ephesians 4:15). In his classic statement on love, he begins by declaring: "If I speak in the tongues of mortals and of angels, but do not have love, I am a noisy gong or a clanging cymbal…", or just so much noise (I Corinthians 13:1).

In more recent times, Mohandas K. Gandhi, and others who have followed in his path, have added their voices in support of this unity of truth and love. In the context of Gandhi's Indian culture, he named his movement *Satyagraha,* meaning "the Force which is born of Truth and Love or non-violence…" Gandhi linked *Satya,* meaning Truth, with *Ahimsa,* meaning Love. For him, the two are so "intertwined that it is practically impossible to disentangle and separate them.

They are like the two sides of a coin," which create a powerful Force (*agraha*) for good.³ For Gandhi this meant, among other things, that he needed to develop and maintain positive relationships with the very people he opposed on issues. His interest was not to destroy the opponent, but to convert the opponent to truth.

Gandhi's further reframing of love as "civility" is also helpful. Civility, he declared, means more than "the mere outward gentleness of speech cultivated for the occasion, but an inborn gentleness and desire to do the opponent good." When opposed, that can be particularly challenging. Indeed, Gandhi observed: "Experience has taught me that civility is the most difficult part of Satyagraha."⁴

In brief, then, Jesus's teaching about truth speaking is foundational for building strong communities. So, let your "yes" be "yes" and your "no" be "no" with such clarity and consistency that the crutch of swearing becomes irrelevant. Trust, essential for quality life together, grows when we consistently and unwaveringly speak truth to each other. And when truth is spoken in love—with respect and civility—community is further strengthened.

Transformative, Relational Justice (the Fifth in the Series)

> Jesus said:
> You have heard that it was said, "An eye for an eye and a tooth for a tooth." But I say to you, Do not resist an evildoer. But if anyone strikes you on the right cheek, turn the other also; and if anyone wants to sue you and take your coat, give your cloak as well; and if anyone forces you to go one mile, go also the second mile. Give to everyone who begs from you, and do not refuse anyone who wants to borrow from you (Matthew 5:38-42).

In this fifth of his fulfillment sayings, Jesus addresses the concern for justice in cases of personal injury. The traditional rule, fully stated in the Mosaic Law as a "life for life, eye for eye, tooth for tooth, hand for hand, foot for foot, burn for burn, wound for wound, stripe for stripe", legitimate demands for equal compensation (Exodus 21:23-25). But Jesus now says, "Do not resist an evildoer…" But is that what he really says?

Earlier King James translators rendered Jesus's words as "resist not evil," leading to the concept of nonresistance. But more recently, as in *The Complete Gospels*, Jesus's words are translated as "don't react violently against the one who is evil."

Biblical scholar Walter Wink finds warrant for this later translation in his analysis of the Greek word commonly translated as "resist" in this passage. The word "is *antistenai*, meaning literally to stand (*stenai*) against (*anti*)." Wink observes that in the Greek version of the Hebrew Bible, *antistenai* is most often used in reference to warfare. Thus the Greek word translated into English as "resist" carries with it the connotation of violence.[5]

Given this understanding, it is not a question of whether one resists evil or not; rather, it is a question of whether one chooses to resist violently, or through other means. Resisting evil, after all, is a core theme of the entire Bible. And Jesus surely resisted evil in his life. Indeed, in his beginning temptations in the wilderness, he resisted Satan himself, as previously noted. And in his ministry he dramatically resisted the demons inhabiting humans by casting them out. His climactic crucifixion and resurrection, moreover, were understood by New Testament Christians as a culminating victory over evil. So it would seem to be out of character for Jesus to teach his followers that they should not resist. "Resist the devil, and he will flee from you," was the Apostle James's later view of the matter (James 4:7).

How, then, is one to understand Jesus's subsequent examples of turning the other cheek when struck on the right, giving more than is demanded when sued, going the second mile when conscripted to go one, and giving to those who beg? Clearly, Jesus is changing the traditional demand for equivalent compensation, as in "an eye for an eye and a tooth for a tooth," to voluntarily giving more than is demanded or taken. But toward what end?

Jesus presents this formula change without comment as to possible outcomes of such radical responses, as though these are simply the right things to do. Subsequent New Testament writings affirm, as in "See that none of you repays evil for evil, but always seek to do good to one another and to all" (1 Thessalonians 5:15), and "Do not repay evil for evil or abuse for abuse; but, on the contrary, repay with a blessing" (I Peter 3:9).

As in the case of Jesus's parables, nevertheless, we may guess that his hearers suspected hidden meanings in these examples, even as the Apostle Paul later saw such teachings as both affirmations and extensions of the tradition. Paul wrote:

> Do not repay anyone evil for evil, but take thought for what is noble in the sight of all. If it is possible, so far as it depends on you, live peaceably with all. Beloved, never avenge yourselves, but leave room for the wrath of God; for it is written, "Vengeance is mine, I will repay, says the Lord." No, "if your enemies are hungry, feed them; if they are thirsty, give them something to drink; for by doing this you will heap burning coals on their heads." Do not be overcome by evil, but overcome evil with good (Romans 12:17-21).

Like Paul, we can surmise that Jesus's hearers, too, would have remembered the teaching of the tradition about leaving vengeance to God. Furthermore, those more alert may well have noticed that Jesus's examples fall into the same genre as the ancient proverb concerning giving food and drink to hungry and thirsty enemies. Some, indeed, may have recalled an actual incident from their history in which a former king of theirs had made "a great feast" for his invading enemy neighbors who had been delivered into his hands. Instead of following the Cain path of killing them, which he could have, he had heaped coals of fire on his enemies' heads, as the proverb states, by feeding them and giving them drink. In this case the result was positive, as it stopped the invasions (2 Kings 6:8-23).

Heaping burning coals on another's head sounds drastic, and has a punitive ring to it. Scholars have puzzled over its meaning. Biblical scholar Gordon M. Zerbe has observed that "the meaning of 'heaping coals of fire' has confronted interpreters from the patristic period until today." Zerbe further notes that "in modern interpretation the majority view holds that the 'coals of fire' refer to the pangs of shame and guilt which lead to repentance."[6]

The Apostle Paul himself follows his reference to the proverb with the principle of "overcoming evil with good," suggesting thereby that the intended outcome of a strategy of goodness is indeed the repentance of the wrongdoer. Such sought for repentance is consistent with Jesus's declaration that God's intention was not to condemn or destroy the world through him, but to save the world (John 3:17).

Taking these interpretive cues, we may frame the question behind Jesus's teaching in his Sermon as follows: How best might the evil of personal injury be addressed so that rather than resorting to violence, evil may be overcome with goodness, particularly in worse-case and seemingly hopeless situations of unequal power?

Jesus's examples are drawn from the everyday experiences of his hearers. The first is a setting involving subordinates and masters or managers, as in a workplace – "if anyone strikes you on the right cheek, turn the other also." The second is a setting in which a person is unjustly sued—"if anyone wants to sue you and take your coat, give your cloak as well." The third is a setting involving locals and a foreign, occupying military force, who could conscript locals to carry their loads but within the limit of one mile—"if anyone forces you to go one mile, go also the second mile." And the fourth is a setting in which persons are the object of begging and borrowing—"give to everyone who begs from you, and do not refuse anyone who wants to borrow from you." We can assume that Jesus's listeners, ordinary folks from the villages and towns of his region, would have quickly identified with one or more of these situations.

The thread that runs through all of Jesus's examples is a change in the formula of "an eye for an eye." Rather than countering an injustice with proportional responses or demands, Jesus commends voluntarily giving more than has been taken or is being demanded— the other cheek, a last piece of clothing, a second mile—and giving to beggars and borrowers.

Furthermore, like sparkling diamonds with many facets, these responses reveal a rich set of dynamics. Seen through the lens of conflict dynamics, Jesus's proposals counter the usual uncontrolled escalation of conflict which results when people respond in kind. His proposals break the cycle of tit for tat, in which each tat tends to evoke a greater tit. Involved is a kind of conflict jujitsu in which direct blows are deflected, requiring different responses. The cycle of uncontrolled escalation is broken, creating the opportunity for more fruitful exchanges.

This redirection may also be understood as an act of leadership. Those who set agendas have power. Turning the cheek, giving up one's last piece of clothing, and going the second mile are assertive acts of agenda setting. They are anything but passive. Unlike an in-kind response which follows the lead of the oppressor, these surprising alternative responses set a new direction. The one oppressed is in effect asserting: "You are now in my court. What are you going to do?" A thoughtful response is more likely in this case then when the conflict has been escalated by in-kind responses.

The given examples may also be understood as similar to parables. A parable is a cool form of communication, to draw on the typology of Marshall McLuhan. Hot forms come in high definition, as in a declaration, command or lecture. Cool forms invite the participation of the other to interpret or complete the message. Feeding hungry enemies, turning the other cheek, going the second mile and giving one's last piece of clothing are all cool responses, inasmuch as they require the recipient of these behaviors to discern their intent and meaning. The victim's unexpected response must now be considered by the offender, as the interpretation and response to a parable must be discerned by its hearer.

Biblical interpreter Walter Wink has interpreted these examples in more confrontational terms. Imagine, to begin with, a workplace in which a worker has not performed to the satisfaction of the owner or manager. A backhand slap, which is required to hit someone on the "right cheek," would be understood in Jesus's cultural context as a blow to "insult, humiliate, degrade," as Walter Wink, among others, has noted. Such backhand slaps in Jesus's time were reserved for use with inferiors. To turn the other cheek was to make a case for equality, for "only equals fought with fists," as would be required to hit the other's left cheek. And "the last thing the master wishes to do is to establish this underling's equality."[7]

In the second case of being sued, the one sued is advised by Jesus to "give your cloak as well" along with the already taken outer garment. As Wink again interprets, when one is being sued and all is taken but one's cloak, voluntarily giving yet one's cloak and so standing naked in court has a way of embarrassing the plaintiff and court into awareness of an injustice.

In the third case of a person being coerced into carrying the pack of occupying Roman soldiers for the established limit of one mile, voluntarily going the second mile creates an awkward situation for the soldier, because he is put into the vulnerable position of violating the military code.[8]

As Wink interprets, the proposed responses to these first three situations have a more confrontational edge than may at first appear. They are clearly not passive. Rather, they call attention to the injustice being perpetrated. Indirectly, they constitute a creative and nonviolent appeal for justice, but they do so with responses of strong and assertive goodness rather than adding harm to harm.

Jesus's fourth and final tactic of giving "to everyone who begs from you" and not refusing "anyone who wants to borrow from you" changes the focus from victim to benefactor. How do those who have relate to those who have not? Unequal distribution of resources in the world existed in Jesus's time, as it has in all time. What, then, constitutes a just and fair distribution of resources in this world? It is telling that in the story of chief tax collector Zacchaeus, making things right with those he may have defrauded was not his only response. He first offered to give half of his possessions to the poor.

In brief, then, Jesus's proposed tactics are not acts of nonresistance, if understood as passivity. Rather, they are acts of resistance by means other than violence. As means, they work in moral, nonviolent ways to secure the attention and awaken the consciences of the unjust. They replace powerful human drives to "get even" as in vengeance, or demand as much as has been taken as in proportional justice. Yet, they are responses that do not give up on justice. Evil is to be overcome, but by means other than violence.

"An Eye for an Eye" Today

Modern systems of justice and discipline have continued in the tradition of proportional justice as reflected in "an eye for an eye." But in contemporary justice systems of the state and discipline systems in schools and other institutions, the primary focus has shifted from compensation to punishment. The principle of proportionality, however, remains, as in "the punishment must fit the crime," or the misdeed. As noted in chapter 1, legal scholar William Ian Miller has observed regarding justice systems of the state, we continue to "worry about proportionality within a grid of punishments." Mostly this "comes down to assigning various numbers of years [in prison] to different offenses depending on their badness, years thus providing the means and measure of payment, rather than eyes, teeth, lives, or money."[9]

Moreover, when proportional sentences have been handed down, the assumption is that justice has been served, even though victims, in particular, have been marginalized in the process and things have not been made right between offender and victim. Once caught in this understanding of justice, frustrated publics tend to press for the severest punishments possible, including such measures as "zero tolerance" discipline systems, in the hope that this will curb evil in the world.

Beginning with the last decades of the twentieth century, nevertheless, restorative justice movements have begun to reclaim justice as a process of making things right between victims and offenders, and redirecting wrongdoers into right and just behaviors and relationships. While often new to contemporaries, many of the means being used in these movements are actually a return to earlier times, not only in terms of Genesis as reflected in the culminating story of Joseph and his brothers, along with the later teachings of Jesus, but often also to how it has been in traditional cultures. Recent works such as *Justice as Healing: Indigenous Ways* (2005), edited by Wanda D. McCaslin, provide an overview of traditional practices that focus strongly on the healing of relationships rather than punishment.

Such talk, moreover, is not entirely foreign to modern ears. Robert Fulghum, as one example, has declared that "all I really need to know about how to live and what to do and how to be I learned in kindergarten." He bears witness that in kindergarten he learned, among other things, to:

Share everything,
Play fair.
Don't hit people.
Put things where you found them.
Clean up your own mess.
Don't take things that aren't yours.
Say you're sorry when you hurt somebody.[10]

Inherent in Fulghum's kindergarten learnings is the basic understanding that persons are responsible for their behaviors and need to make things right when they have harmed another. However, when wrongs escalate to the level of crimes, in modern systems of criminal justice the primary relationship between offender and victim is preempted by the state. The state then throws up roadblocks to restorative communication in the context of primary communities. Wrongdoers are separated, not only from those they have wronged, but also the primary communities to which they rightly should be accountable.

While this separation may be well intentioned in order to prevent further harm to victims and protect offenders from escalated vengeance, rigid enforcement of the separation closes the door to the possibility of restoration. The frustration which this breeds is well expressed in the last words of Napoleon Beazley, an offender who was executed in Texas on May 28, 2002. His story is told by Robert K. Elder in *Last Words of the Executed.* In high school Beazley had been a star athlete and president of his senior class. But he had gotten involved with drugs, and within time committed a murder. In his last words before being executed, he stated: "The act I committed to put me here was not just heinous, it was senseless. But the person that committed that act is no longer here—I am."

Speaking, then, of others like him on death row, Beazley pleaded before he died: "Give those men a chance to do what's right. Give them a chance to undo their wrongs. A lot of them want to fix the mess they started, but don't know how. The problem is not in that people aren't willing to help find out, but in the system telling them it won't matter anyway. No one wins tonight. No one gets closure. No one walks away victorious."[11]

Though modern justice systems close doors to persons like Beazley, Robert Fulghum's witness to what he learned in kindergarten suggests that the core value, expressed simply as you should "say you're sorry when you hurt somebody," has not been lost, even to persons on death row. What has been lost are the means of giving voice and feet to this value.

Advocates of the growing movement toward restorative justice call for a change in our justice paradigm; that is, to change the lenses through which we see, to use the metaphor of Howard Zehr, pioneering restorative justice advocate.[12] Rather than simply executing the Beazleys of the world who no longer are what they were, other doors might be opened to restore such to community in the best traditions of the village and historic religious teachings, such as those of Jesus.

New lenses will help us see opportunities for bringing willing victims and offenders together in safe, controlled settings of mediation, family group conferencing, sentencing circles, and the like, in order to make things right. Further surrounding victims with support groups, and offenders with accountability groups drawn from extended families, faith communities and the larger civil society will more likely nurture them to wholeness than incarcerating offenders with like-minded wrongdoers.

Restorative justice movements exemplify the spirit and teachings of Jesus. His sermonic examples may be taken as suggestive seeds from which many varieties may be grown. His vision is of a world in which just and righteous living is the norm. He came, as I have noted, not "to condemn the world, but in order that the world might be saved through him" (John 3:17).

Jesus's vision, furthermore, offers a fuller loaf to victims. "An eye for an eye and a tooth for a tooth," and their offspring, are but half a loaf, often leaving victims marginalized and less than satisfied. A full loaf requires the restoration of *shalom*, or peace, and that requires the addition of further ingredients such as confession, forgiveness, restitution, and direction-changing repentance, as we earlier saw modeled in the story of Joseph and his brothers. Among even the most grievous offenders, there are those who actually seek peace, as Napoleon Beazley's story illustrates. And though Beazley was told that making things right with those harmed no longer mattered for those on death row, Jesus knew that it does matter. Fulfilling the state's sentence is one thing. Making peace with those one has actually harmed is another.

Conclusion

In brief, then, as a good neighbor, speak truth that inspires trust, and seek justice that restores, for these are the pathways to healthy neighborhoods and communities. In pursuit of justice, leave vengeance to God and flee violence. Simultaneously, do not be passive, but be assertive in setting the agenda by surprising the unjust through alternative responses of goodness, and opening doors of restorative, healing justice for both victims and offenders. So will peace be at home in our neighborhoods and communities.

BEST PRACTICE
Truth and Justice

As I write, truth is an endangered species. Trust, its companion, dies with it. And community, which depends on both, is diminished. We travel alone. Impersonal media and unethical leaders make it easier to diminish truth and justice, Accountability for speaking falsehoods becomes more difficult and vigilante justice contribute to endangering both. Sayings, such as "I cannot lie," attributed to George Washington upon cutting down a cherry tree, though mythical, fade into oblivion, no longer having the force they once had. When a child in the middle of the twentieth century, lying and foul language were causes for having one's mouth washed out with soap. Handshakes were known to be sufficient to seal a deal. One's word was to be trusted. Today, Jesus's first century call to "let your yes be yes and your no be no" as a best practice is as relevant as ever. Justice as punishment has become so deeply rooted that it has tended to become an end in itself. Focus often is on what punishment would be adequate as payment for a crime, rather than on possibilities for restoration. Nevertheless, as I write there has been an awakening of the possibility of justice that restores. Biblical injunctions to "turn the other cheek" and surprise one's enemy with food and drink suggest best practices that have the potential to waken the perpetrator of injustice to the meaning of true justice. Restoring such to community remains a noble goal, challenging though that may be. Victim-offender mediation, community mediation centers, circles of support for recently released prisoners, restorative family and school discipline systems, alternative dispute resolution, and the like represent best practices that have been emerging. All also represent possibilities for everyday best practices in our families, workplaces, neighborhoods, churches, friendship groups, communities, and the like.

CHAPTER 9
Transformative Pathways for Enemies

ANCIENT HEADLINES
(as they might have appeared in today's media)

Love for Enemies Proclaimed by Hillside Preacher

God Set Forth as Model for How to Treat Enemies

Ancient Proverb About Feeding Enemies Resurrected

"Overcome Evil with Good" Advocated as Strategy

TODAY'S HEADLINES
(as they have appeared in today's media)

What? Love my enemy!
Manila Bulletin, February 18, 2011

Members at Ground Zero overcome evil with good
The Forensic Examiner, January 1, 2003

To be reconciled: Vietnam veteran returns and embraces former enemies
Sunday Gazette-Mail, July 5, 2000

Palestinians Practice Nonviolent Resistance In Bilin
NPR Morning Edition, December 29, 2009

Several Congolese colleagues and I traveled by ferry across peaceful and scenic Lake Kivu dividing Rwanda from Eastern Congo. We had boarded the ferry in Goma, and after several hours approached Bukavu at the opposite end of the lake. It was late afternoon. As I stood on the open deck with Pascal Kulungu, Congolese friend who had studied in my California university, we both had the same thought. Approaching the city laid out on the hills before us was like approaching the grandeur of San Francisco from its bay, also on a ferry, as both of us had experienced. At moments such as this, I have pondered how places of such beauty, known in this case also as the Switzerland of Africa, could generate such violence. More than five million are estimated to have died since 1996 as a result of the wars in the Democratic Republic of Congo, concentrated mostly in this beautiful eastern region.

Later, we traveled into the luscious, green covered hills surrounding Bukavu to the region of Walunga. There, in the Walunga regional hospital, we watched as women who had been raped during the Congo wars movingly re-enacted their experiences. We then stopped at a communal hut in a nearby village crowded with other women who also had been raped during the ongoing conflicts. They spun out sad tales of what had happened to them. We listened, mostly in silence, overwhelmed by the tragedy of it all.

Theologian Miroslav Volf has well expressed the tension one feels when one encounters such violence. He begins his seminal book, *Exclusion and Embrace,* by noting his very personal challenge when asked whether as a Croat he could embrace Serbian fighters who during the Balkan crisis of the 1990s "had been sowing desolation in my native country, herding people into concentration camps, raping women, burning down churches, and destroying cities." Volf describes being "pulled in two different directions by the blood of the innocent crying out to God and by the blood of God's Lamb offered for the guilty."[1]

That Jesus Lamb experienced similar pulls. Zealots of his time pulled in the direction of violence to drive out their hated Roman occupiers. Even Jesus's very own disciples saw him as the means for delivering them from their enemy outsiders. But there was also a different pull. This pull is summarized in the sixth and final saying in Jesus's fulfillment series. Here Jesus states:

> You have heard that they were told, "Love your **neighbour** and hate your **enemy**." But what I tell you is this: Love your enemies and pray for your persecutors; only so can you be children of your heavenly Father, who causes the sun to rise on good and bad alike, and sends the rain on the innocent and the wicked. If you love only those who love you, what reward can you expect? Even the tax-collectors do as much as that. If you greet only your **brothers**, what is there extraordinary about that? Even the heathen do as much. There must be no limit to your goodness, as your heavenly Father's goodness knows no bounds
> (Matthew 5:43-48; REB, bold mine).

The Greek word translated as "goodness" in the above Revised English Bible version is *teleios*. "Goodness," unlike the more frequent translation of *teleios* as "perfect," better retains the logic of the passage. For it is the goodness of God, "who causes the sun to rise on good and bad alike, and sends the rain on the innocent and the wicked," that Jesus sets forth as model. For Jesus, following the example of God in also extending goodness to enemies is the summit of moral development. In this he is consistent with his tradition, which in the Torah centers ethics in the character of God: "Be holy, for I [God] am holy" (e.g. Leviticus 11:44-45).

This summit of love and goodness toward enemies, moreover, rises yet above the prior circles of family and neighbor. While speaking of enemies, Jesus references the former, as highlighted in bold in the text above. Now, however, Jesus suggests that greeting a brother or sister and loving those who love us are universal practices, and so surely not extraordinary. And who in his Jewish audience would not have understood love for neighbor as a core teaching of their Torah? But as to the enemy, his hearers had gotten it wrong. Love, not hate, is to be normative. The summit cannot be attained without yet embracing the enemy. That is the final challenge.

The Circle of the Enemy

Who is my enemy? No record exists that this clarifying, boundary question was ever asked of Jesus. No lawyer seems to have come along to ask the question, as in the case of the neighbor.

Perhaps the question did not need to be asked. Jesus's hearers had a long history of enemies. Among them were enemy empires that had conquered their land, and taken their people into captivity. Now they were occupied by yet another enemy—the hated Roman Empire. Likewise, their Psalms were filled with references to personal enemies. Jesus's hearers had experienced many varieties of enemies, even as today enemies are personal, social, tribal, ethnic, racial, religious, organizational, political, national, international and more.

Excluding certain categories of enemies as beyond the reach of Jesus's love, prayer and nonviolent practices has been a common human phenomenon. Several examples follow.

Personal vs Social-Political Enemies

Some interpreters have considered Jesus's enemy teachings as simply not practical or workable in social, political, international and like situations. These interpreters have limited his teaching to personal enemies.

Martin Luther King, Jr. confesses to having once owned such an interpretation. In his "Pilgrimage to Nonviolence," he writes: "The turn-the-other-cheek and the love-your-enemies philosophies are valid, I felt, only when individuals are in conflict with other individuals; when racial groups and nations are in conflict, a more realistic approach is necessary." But then, he reports, "I was introduced to the life and teachings of Mahatma Gandhi." Like the outsider Samaritan in Jesus's parable of the Good Samaritan, it was outsider Gandhi who modeled for King how to practice what Jesus taught. King put it succinctly: "Christ furnished the spirit and motivation and Gandhi furnished the method."[2] Christian theologian John Howard Yoder further observes: "It was thanks to the loner Tolstoy and the outsider Gandhi that the churchman Martin Luther King, Jr....was able to bring Jesus' word on violence back into the churches."[3]

Among those who helped King understand Jesus through Gandhi was E. Stanley Jones, twentieth-century Christian missionary to India and early American biographer of Gandhi. Jones himself had earlier been compelled to do his own rethinking. He reports that "when Gandhi was about to begin the noncooperation movement [in India], I was skeptical about it." Jones wrote a letter to Gandhi "begging him not to begin it," fearing "violence and bloodshed and chaos." Gandhi responded with what Jones describes as an "amazing letter" assuring him that he would "not begin the civil disobedience movement without careful thought, without proper precautions, and, what is more, without copious praying." Gandhi, moreover, invited Jones to pray with him. Jones then reports that "my objections melted away when I saw it in action—hot-tempered men and women taking suffering, not giving it; submitting to their heads being cracked under blows from lathis (long metal-tipped bamboo poles); going to jail without a protest; asking for the severest penalty, as in the case of Gandhi himself; and as they were led out of court to prison, saying to the British judge: 'Father, forgive them; they know not what they do.' Hindus saying that to the Christian! 'We now know what you mean by the cross—we are bearing it,' said a Hindu to me one day."[4]

Following the social and political turmoil of the 1950s and 1960s, insider Christian theologian John Howard Yoder determined to make his own investigation of the teachings of Jesus. Given his observed inclinations to judge Jesus's teachings as socially irrelevant, he posed as his central question: "Is there here [in the Gospel accounts of the life and teachings of Jesus] a social ethic?" Based on his examination, he concluded that, indeed, what Jesus taught is "not only relevant but also normative for a contemporary Christian social ethic."

Yoder's work, published as *The Politics of Jesus* (1972), has become a foundational work in Christian social ethics. Others have since followed Yoder's lead, confirming that Jesus indeed had something to say not only about how we act as individuals, but also collectively in our faith and social-political *ekklesias*, or communities.

Enemies Defined as Subhuman or Nonhuman

In 1938, Walter Buch, the supreme judge of the German Nazi party, wrote: "The National Socialist has recognized [that] the Jew is not a human being."[5] The German word is *Untermensch*, meaning "subhuman." So defined, it is no problem to seize an infant by the legs in one hand and shoot out her brain with a pistol in the other. Or, to herd persons so defined as vermin into gas chambers. More recently, in the Rwandan genocide of the 1990s, tribal Tutsis were similarly dehumanized by Hutu propagandists who called them *"Inyenzi*, or 'cockroaches.'"

While aggressors may define those they are seeking to eliminate as subhuman or nonhuman, victims in turn may also so view their enemy oppressors. Even leaders and people of faith are so tempted when their own people are victimized, or they see great evil in the other. Though words such as *Untermensch* or *Inyenzi* may not be used, the disrespect shown through actions betray a similar dehumanization of the other. Richard J. Mouw, when president of Fuller Theological Seminary, noted that "as a Christian I…worry that many believers seem to be contributing more to the problem than to the solution. Well-known clergy tell their followers that the time has come for a 'battle' against the forces of unbelief. The TV cameras show Christians on the picket lines, angrily shaking their fists at their opponents. We are often good examples of the kind of difficult people whom [the poet] Yeats described as being 'full of passionate intensity'."[6] Mouw proceeded to explore the alternative of what he calls "convicted civility," observing that embracing the other as human need not result in giving up one's convictions. One can be strongly convicted while still embracing the other as human.

On April 1, 1982, my wife and I attended a meeting at the Tantur Ecumenical Center near Jerusalem in Israel. Simha Flapan, leader in Jewish-Arab relations, who had been a personal friend of the influential twentieth-century Jewish philosopher Martin Buber, was a major contributor. Reflecting on his mid-twentieth-century Middle East work promoting dialogue between Arabs and Jews, he told the story of how one day, in great frustration, he had come to Buber with the question: "How do you have a discussion with Arabs when they always walk out when Jews show up?" Buber, noted for his teachings on dialogue, responded: "To have a dialogue you don't need Arab presence, only Arab existence." Puzzled for a moment, I nevertheless quickly recalled Buber's teaching about different levels of inclusion. The foundational first level is the recognition of the legitimacy of the other's existence. Buber proposed as example "a disputation between two men, thoroughly different in nature and outlook and calling, where in an instant—as by the action of a messenger as anonymous as he is invisible—it happens that each is aware of the other's full legitimacy, wearing the insignia of necessity and of meaning. What an illumination!"[7] Whereas "presence" is surely desirable, even more basic for Buber is the recognition of the legitimacy of the other's existence. Dialogue depends on this beginning recognition. Though this illumination may come from an anonymous and invisible messenger, it surely expresses what is core to the biblical tradition; namely, that even those most unlike us, including enemies, are also created in the image of God, and so are both legitimate and to be valued.

Journalist Lance Morrow recognized this essential truth in *Time* magazine's lead story on its selection of opposing leaders—-Yitzhak Rabin and Yasser Arafat in the Middle East and Nelson Mandela and F.W. De Klerk in South Africa— as their "men of the year" for 1993. In that year, "it was against all the usual inclinations of the war devils that these four men took what must be the first step in the metaphysics of peace, they recognized the other's existence. They crossed the line from the primitive intransigences of blood/color/tribe to the logic of tolerance and, farther down the road, of civil society."[8]

In 1981 Roger Fisher and William Ury of the Harvard Negotiation Project published *Getting to Yes*, which arguably became the most widely read work of the time on the practice of negotiation.[9] Even Mikhail Gorbachev had a copy in his Kremlin library during the last days of the Soviet Union. One of four cardinal principles Fisher and Ury set forth for successful negotiation is to "separate the people from the problem;" that is, treat people as people and problems as problems. Inferred is the humanity of the other.

Bill Richardson, former chief U.S. representative to the United Nations, has reflected on how to talk with the "world's toughest leaders," including the worst dictators. As reported by Tad Szulc, Richardson observes: "You have to be a human being. You cannot be arrogant or condescending... If you treat each individual with respect, each nation with dignity, you can get a lot further than trying to muscle them."[10]

Though I may believe that including my enemies as human should be rooted in principle rather than outcomes, I can also celebrate that such an approach is effective. So I cite the preceding as examples of contemporary secular wisdom that is a variation of biblical wisdom. All humans, however evil, are created in the image of God, and deserving of our care and respect, not for what they do, but who they are. Love and prayer for enemies presumes their humanity. For Jesus, the problem is evil, surely never to be excused. But no sub-circles of enemies are to be dehumanized and so excluded from the reach of love and prayer.

Jesus's Ethic for Enemies

Jesus instructed his hearers to love their enemies and pray for their persecutors. Such *agape* love, as it is called in Greek, is expressed in concrete behaviors, as described by the Apostle Paul.

Love is patient; love is kind; love is not envious or boastful or arrogant or rude. It does not insist on its own way; it is not irritable or resentful; it does not rejoice in wrongdoing, but rejoices in the truth. It bears all things, believes all things, hopes all things, endures all things (I Corinthians 13:4-7).

Treating enemies accordingly is particularly challenging.

In calling his hearers to practice such love, Jesus echoed Joseph of Genesis, who in the early, extracanonical *Testament of Joseph*, is reported to have said: "And if any one seeketh to do evil unto you, do well unto him, and pray for him, and ye shall be redeemed of the Lord from all evil."[11] New Testament scholar John E. Toews has observed: "Joseph was the model of...non-retaliation in Judaism; Jesus in the early church."[12]

In his Sermon, however, it is God, "who causes the sun to rise on good and bad alike, and sends the rain on the innocent and the wicked," that Jesus sets forth as model. By way of imitation, then, "there must be no limit to your goodness, as your heavenly Father's goodness knows no bounds." The Apostle Paul later summarized: "Do not be overcome by evil, but overcome evil with good" (Romans 12:21).

Practices of Goodness

Whatever image of God Jesus's hillside congregation may have derived from their Hebrew Scriptures and oral traditions, it was the goodness of God that Jesus lifted up for emulation. If, then, the goodness of love and prayer, as the goodness of the sun and rain, is also to be extended to enemies, we may presume that practices previously proposed for families and neighbors, too, would extend to enemies. Beyond refusing to cooperate with evil, seeking peace with enemies in the Jesus way would then seem also to begin by inviting enemies into conversation. And when resistance is encountered, stepwise escalation may follow as with an erring brother or sister. Likewise, an enemy may also lead one to greater truths, a possibility to which one must remain open. Gandhi understood this, as he invited his occupying British enemies into a process of mutual truth seeking.

One might argue, moreover, that the foregoing represent nothing unique, but simply represent the way of the wise. Not only wise persons, but also wise communities and nations seek initially to resolve conflicts through negotiation. Such negotiation, moreover, works best when not of an "eye for an eye" variety, but principled, as confirmed, for example, by those associated with the Harvard Negotiation Project. Roger Fisher and Scott Brown of the Project, for instance, advocate "an unconditionally constructive strategy." As noted in part one of this work, as I now repeat, they propose six concrete guidelines for negotiators, all of which assume, as Jesus taught, that one does not respond in kind to non-constructive behaviors.

1. **Rationality.** Even if they are acting emotionally, balance emotions with reason.
2. **Understanding.** Even if they misunderstand us, try to understand them.
3. **Communication.** Even if they are not listening, **consult them before deciding** on matters that affect them.
4. **Reliability.** Even if they are trying to deceive us, neither trust them nor deceive them; be reliable.
5. **Noncoercive modes of influence.** Even if they are trying to coerce us, neither yield to that coercion nor try to coerce them; be open to persuasion and try to persuade them.
6. **Acceptance.** Even if they reject us and our concerns as unworthy of their consideration, **accept them as worthy of our consideration, care about them, and be open to learning from them.**[13]

Fisher and Brown then conclude: "These guidelines are not advice on how to be 'good,' but rather on how to be effective." Or, as we may reframe their conclusion, they are both good and effective.

We may also take Fisher and Brown's formulation as a contemporary expansion of negotiation modeled by Abraham in dealing with his nephew Lot. As earlier described, Abraham was firm, clear, polite and generous.

As to further stepwise escalation when negotiations falter, others who are wise have also been helpful. Nonviolent options for escalation are many. Political scientist Gene Sharp, in his seminal *The Politics of Nonviolent Action: Part Two* (1973), identifies 198 different possibilities. Jesus's stepwise model in Matthew 18, then, may be taken as a beginning seed which has grown into many varieties. Positive outcomes of such escalations, moreover, seem to be built into the very fabric of the universe, even if not guaranteed.

There is reason to rejoice, then, when such nonviolent practices find their way into the public arena, though motivations may vary, as illustrated by the historic "velvet revolutions" of 1989. As one example, British historian Timothy Garton Ash has noted that the Information Bulletin of the Czech Civic Forum declared on December 2, 1989: "Let us refuse any form of terror and violence [in opposition to the existing Communist regime]. Our weapons are love and nonviolence." Then Ash adds: "In the case of Pope John Paul II and of Aung San Suu Kyi and other Burmese Buddhists, one can say that the choice of peaceful means was primarily a moral and religious one. 'Defeat evil with good!' was the Polish Pope's often repeated message. In most cases, however, this is a strategic rather than a moral choice—and none the worse for that."[14]

Whatever the motivation, it is true that nonviolent movements have had a high degree of success, not only in the velvet revolutions of 1989 leading to the end of the Soviet empire, but also in a longer history as revealed in a comparative study of violent and nonviolent social-political movements between 1900 and 2006 authored by international scholars Erica Chenoweth and Maria J. Stephan (2011). Their comparative study led them to the conclusion that throughout the last century until 2006, the last year included in their study, "nonviolent resistance campaigns were nearly twice as likely to achieve full or partial success as their violent counterparts."[15]

Motivations, nevertheless, do make a difference. Whereas one may choose nonviolence for strategic rather than moral reasons, the danger of simply a strategic choice is that one may more easily return to violence when that seems advantageous. For Jesus, the choice was rooted in principle. The character of God, as articulated in his Sermon, was the model to be imitated. And in a broader application of stepwise thinking, his ministry as a whole was shaped by stepwise teaching and demonstrations of power in casting out demons, healing the sick, feeding the hungry, calming the storm, giving sight to the blind, and raising the dead. These were all acts of goodness confirming the reign of God on earth. The cumulative effect was that many received him gladly, yet there were those who persisted in resisting. Among those who resisted were those in power, both religiously and politically. As resistance escalated, the stage was set for a final confrontation.

When All Else Fails

What does one do, then, when all of the forgoing fail to overcome evil, particularly if one is not willing that any should perish, as Jesus stated his goal? How far did the "unlimited goodness" of God extend for Jesus?

The story, perhaps fictional, is told of a fellow who turned the other cheek, as Jesus commanded, but then proceeded to demolish his opponent because Jesus hadn't said what to do next. But, then, he did have more to say. But so have others.

Carl von Clausewitz (1780-1831), in his classic and influential treatise on war, describes war as "politics by other means." One option when all else fails, then, is to escalate to war; that is, to inflict "human suffering through violence" on those who persist in resisting, as John Keegan, British military historian, describes war's "engine of change."[16] While Clausewitz and Keegan speak of war, the same may be said of escalated conflict in the home and neighborhood. When frustration peaks, escalation to violence is an option in all human relationships.

But there is also another "politics by [still] other means," as in *The Politics of Jesus*, to recall the title of John Howard Yoder's illumination of the social-political teachings and example of Jesus. Both politics by other means were part of Jesus's inheritance: the warrior tradition of the Exodus and the conquest of ancient Palestine, on one hand, and the later "suffering servant" tradition enunciated by the eighth century BCE prophet Isaiah, on the other. Both traditions share a beginning approach of conversation and stepwise escalation to effect some change, even as negotiation and stepwise sanctions against enemy nations are used in our time. In the warrior tradition of the Exodus, escalation consisted of a series of plagues. For Jesus it was increasing social power as previously described. But when these fail to produce the desired outcome, again we are left with the question, what does one do?

The failure of the stepwise plagues to free ancient Israel from their bondage in Egypt was climaxed by violence, though in this case the violence of God. In place of God, today leaders and citizens alike resort to violence when escalated strategies and sanctions fail. Their "engine of change," as described by John Keegan, is the "infliction of human suffering through violence."

Jesus, however, modeled the radical alternative earlier set forth by the prophet Isaiah. Isaiah's alternative vision, as described by biblical historian Paul D. Hanson, was that of a God who enters history, "not through the agency of a dazzling king, but through that of a despised and suffering Servant. The new faithful community was to be constituted not through force, but through the depths of divine compassion encountered in obedience unto death."[17]

The prevailing narrative in Israel's history, nevertheless, was that of the Exodus. As Messiah, Jesus's student-disciples expected a Moses, who would again restore the kingdom to Israel. Now occupied, as they were, by the Roman Empire, they were expectantly waiting for another historic moment of deliverance.

When Jesus first spoke to them about the alternative of a suffering servant, forecasting his death and resurrection, his disciples were shocked. All three of the synoptic Gospels record the moment (Matthew 16:21-23; Mark 8:27-33; Luke 9:18-21). His announcement did not fit their paradigm. Peter, leading disciple among Jesus's core group of twelve, quickly took him aside and rebuked him. Jesus returned the rebuke in language that could not have been stronger: "Get behind me, Satan! You are a stumbling block to me; for you are setting your mind not on divine things but on human things." A last temptation of Jesus was to choose violence in support of the national restoration vision held by those closest to him. Again, though pressured, he did not yield.

This dramatic exchange, then, set the direction for all that followed. At this fork in the road, Jesus chose the narrow way of the cross over the broad way of the sword. And as the poet Robert Frost has said about such crossroad choices, "that has made all the difference."

Professing something as a teacher or prophet, nevertheless, is one thing. Following through in terms of personal modeling is another. Jesus had denounced religious leaders of his time who did not practice what they preached. His critique had created enemies. So what would Jesus now actually do as his enemies relentlessly pursued him? Would he respond to them as he taught, or too leave his teaching hollow without personal example? Might he now, when confronted with escalated force, perhaps even revert back to the more primal response of violence, as did the sons of Jacob when their sister Dinah was raped? Or, as some in pragmatic nonviolent movements of our time revert back to violence when confronted with violence? As events began to unfold after arriving with his disciples in Jerusalem for yet another Passover, that national celebration of the warrior God's historic deliverance from Egypt, he was put to the test.

On the night of his arrest, leading disciple Peter, not yet comprehending Jesus's choice, drew his culinary, fish cleaning knife, usually translated as "sword," and in the spirit of holy war whacked off the ear of a servant of the high priest who had come along for the arrest. Once again, Jesus rebuked his slow-learning disciple: "Put your sword back into its place; for all who take the sword will perish by the sword" (Matthew 26:52). In an act of goodness, he then healed the severed ear of the servant.

Furthermore, Jesus said, "Do you think that I cannot appeal to my Father, and he will at once send me more than twelve legions of angels?"—a force that could have numbered more than 80,000 given the varied size of Roman legions at the time. Jesus had options. His choice was not pragmatic, but clearly based on principle. It is one thing pragmatically to choose the way of nonviolence when there are no other options; it is a greater thing to make a principled choice when options are at hand, as Gandhi has observed.[18]

Jesus's rejection of violence was further reinforced when he was subsequently examined by Pilate, who was the regional Roman governor of the occupation. When Pilate asked Jesus whether he was the King of the Jews, he responded: "My kingdom is not from this world. If my kingdom were from this world, my followers would be fighting to keep me from being handed over to the Jews. But as it is, my kingdom is not from here" (John 18:33-38).

Governor Pilate of the Roman Empire and Jesus of the Kingdom of God represent two fundamentally different "engines of change", to use the metaphor of British military historian John Keegan. Both entail the possibility of suffering, but with a difference.

Working for change through violence has resulted in enormous suffering at all levels of human relationships, including families, neighbors and enemies. John Keegan, in an attempt to highlight the suffering caused by war, the extreme manifestation of this approach to change, critiques Clausewitz's classic thesis of war as "the continuation of politics by different means." Keegan, writing as a military historian, considers this thesis as "the most pernicious philosophy of warmaking yet conceived" in its assumption that "war, in short, is a value-free activity, outside the moral sphere," which "is to be limited only by the calculation of the political interest in which it was undertaken in the first place."[19] Yet, as Keegan observes: "In the practice of warmaking it is to the principles of Clausewitz that the statesman and the supreme commander still turn."[20]

Keegan makes no religious argument, but simply notes that "the eye-witness and the historian must flee from Clausewitz's methods" and must record the hot facts of war that "burn with the heat of the fires of hell."[21] War is not morally neutral—simply another amoral means to a political end—whether that end is expressed in what rhetorician Richard M. Weaver has called "god terms" such as freedom, democracy, justice, or otherwise. Enormous suffering has resulted from the use of violence as an engine of change. More than 100 million died as a result of war in the twentieth century alone, not to speak of the additional millions wounded and displaced from their homes.

Yet "overcoming evil with good" has also led to suffering, but with a difference. Prominent among those who have modeled this difference in our time has been Mahatma Gandhi. E. Stanley Jones, early biographer of Gandhi (1948), observes that in opposing the British occupiers of his country, "the weapons Gandhi chose were simple: We will match our capacity to suffer against your capacity to inflict the suffering, our soul force against your physical force. We will not hate you, but we will not obey you. Do what you like, and we will wear you down by our capacity to suffer. And in the winning of the freedom we will so appeal to your heart and conscience that we will win you. So ours will be a double victory; we will win our freedom and our captors in the process."[22]

This manifesto of suffering subsequently influenced Martin Luther King, Jr. As told in the collected *Papers of Martin Luther King, Jr.*, King underlined this quote in his personal copy of Jones's biography of Gandhi, and "made frequent use of it in his discussions of nonviolence." For King, "unearned suffering is redemptive."[23]

In further declaring self-suffering as superior to the infliction of suffering on others, Gandhi observes that as humans we have "done many things which were subsequently found to have been wrong." If earlier, then, we would have been willing to accept self-suffering rather than inflicting suffering on others, at least the others would not have been made to suffer for our errors.[24] The significance of Gandhi's observation is magnified when we think of the immense suffering caused by wars later judged to have been wrong.

Followers of Jesus, nevertheless, have a long history of joining in inflicting suffering on enemies to effect some change. Symbolic is the statue of Ulrich Zwingli, the sixteenth century Swiss Reformation leader, standing before the historic Wasserkirche (water church) in Zurich, Switzerland. While clasping the Bible under one arm, he grasps the sword with both hands.

Unwittingly, Zwingli's linkage of Bible and sword provided inspiration for one of the foremost violent revolutionaries of the twentieth century; namely Vladimir Llyich Lenin. Lenin lived in Zurich prior to the 1917 Russian Revolution. Years before his time, the Wasserkirche had been transformed from a church into a community library. It was Lenin's frequent destination. As he passed the statute of Zwingli on his way, Alexander Solzhenitsyn reports: "Lenin always spared him an approving glance. True, his book was the Bible, but all the same, for the sixteenth century, he had shown splendid resoluteness, today's socialists could learn a lesson from him. An excellent combination, the book and the sword. The book, with the sword as its extension."[25]

For Walter Wink, on the other hand, the sword symbolizes "the Myth of Redemptive Violence." This myth, rooted in ancient creation stories, "enshrines the belief that violence saves, that war brings peace, that might makes right." And when a story is told often enough, as has this story of so-called redemptive violence, it "ceases to be a tale and is accepted as reality itself." As Wink observes, "this Myth of Redemptive Violence is the real myth of the modern world."[26]

Yet, the temptation to resort to violence remains when faced with overwhelming evil and all other measures have failed. Since Augustine, in particular, theories of just war have been spun in an effort to discern when inflicting "human suffering through violence" on others to effect some change may be justified. Christian theologian Miroslav Volf, however, has challenged: "Show me one warring party that does not think its war is just!"[27] Walter Wink further observes:

"No authoritative Christian body has ever, prior to the commencement of fighting, decreed that one side or the other is justified in warfare on the basis of just-war criteria. Instead, the sorry record reveals that Christian churches have usually simply endorsed the side on which they happened to find themselves."[28]

For Eduardus Van der Borght of the VU University Amsterdam, the 1992-95 Bosnian war in the European context provides an example. Though religious leaders in that "heated atmosphere...knew and used the Christian peace and reconciliation vocabulary...these same religious leaders, supported by theologians and lay believers, defined themselves in terms of national or ethnic identities without reserve." He further observes: "Religions desire to present themselves as agents of reconciliation and peace in conflict, but in situations as these in the former Yugoslavia...religious traditions tend to become a party that identifies itself with one side in the conflict and as such become agents of exclusion themselves."[29]

A prime example of the church being seduced by the state in twentieth-century history remains that of Nazi Germany. Whereas German theologian Dietrich Bonhoeffer, like Gandhi in India, sought to create a resisting community, both in Germany through the Confessing Church and globally through the ecumenical movement, neither gained widespread support. Furthermore, Bonhoeffer's own Finkenwalde seminary students yielded to the military draft when called to serve in Hitler's armies, though their study at the seminary had included Bonhoeffer's lectures on the Sermon on the Mount published in 1937 as *Nachfolge,* and later in English translation as *The Cost of Discipleship.* As reported by Eberhard Bethge, friend and early biographer of Bonhoeffer, a few of his former students actually "became officers; others received military decorations. Some were taken prisoner and later sent to compulsory labour camps; others were condemned to death by Soviet courts martial. Most were killed in action." According to Bethge, more than seventy-five of Bonhoeffer's former seminary students lost their lives serving in the Nazi German military.[30]

Had the German and ecumenical church stood united in opposition to Hitler, might what has been called "the last good war" really been necessary? In regard to the Jewish question, Daniel Goldhagen has pointed to various instances in which "the Nazis backed down when faced with serious, widespread popular opposition" on issues of concern. But the extermination of the Jews, for the most part, did not rise to that level. One exception occurred in 1943 when the Nazis in the capital of Berlin rounded up Jews in mixed marriages. Non-Jewish spouses rose up in protest, and the Nazis backed down. Goldhagen concludes: "Had the Nazis been faced with a German populace who saw Jews as ordinary human beings, and German Jews as their brothers and sisters, then it is hard to imagine that the Nazis would have proceeded, or would have been able to proceed, with the extermination of the Jews."[31] Whether Goldhagen is correct or not in his estimation, the reality remains that the church in Germany, for the most part, was of no help, having allowed itself to be co-opted by the state.

In my American context, the predominant Christian response to war as the ultimate engine of change also is to follow the lead of the state, though the state has honored the option of conscientious objection to participation in the military. Nevertheless, with today's volunteer military, Christian participation in the state's wars continues notwithstanding just war considerations or that it was not so in the beginning with Jesus and the early church. American churches that post the American and Christian flags in their sanctuaries give visual witness to their priorities by how they position these flags. Characteristically they follow the national flag code, which dictates that the American flag be positioned in the place of honor in reference to other flags. By inference, then, the church is symbolically positioned in subordination to the nation.

Speaking more globally, Eduardus Van der Borght of the Netherlands observes: "For many Christians, the loyalty to their faith and their church, and the love for their country or people, were, and still are, almost as self-evident as the flipside of one coin," notwithstanding a professed belief in the church as global.[32] It is not a question, however, of whether we should be loyal to our state, as to our families, our places of work, the organizations we belong to, and the like. We all have multiple loyalties, as also did Jesus. Not only did he dance between his family of origin and family of faith, but in regard to the state he famously declared: "Give…to the emperor the things that are the emperor's, and to God the things that are God's" (Matthew 22:21, Mark 12:17, Luke 20:25). For Jesus, the critical question was not one of dancing among many loyalties; rather, it was the question of who led in the dance.

In today's faith communities, nevertheless, the evidence suggests that not only are just war criteria such as protecting civilians in warfare "frail," as political scientist Alexander B. Downes has demonstrated in his study of *Targeting Civilians in War*, but the understanding of religious community, what theologians call "ecclesiology," is also frail. Without a strong sense of religious community as transcending tribal, ethnic, national and like boundaries, in war Catholics of one tribe, ethnicity or country kill even their fellow Catholics in another, Protestants kill Protestants, Jews kill Jews, Muslims kill Muslims, all without rising to the level of discipline in church, synagogue or mosque. One may speak the vocabulary of peace and reconciliation, to use the words of Van der Borght, but betray it in actual practice.

Psychological dissonance theory further suggests that as humans we will always find reasons to justify our behaviors, including exceptions to principles we profess to uphold. We should then not be surprised to hear justifications, not only for dropping bombs of assorted varieties on this or that city, town, village or dwelling, but also for the daily violence in our families and communities.

This proclivity to rationalize our actions as just is what drives even criminal behavior. As psychiatrist James Gilligan has observed, "*the attempt to achieve and maintain justice, or to undo or prevent injustice, is the one and only universal cause of violence.*" Gilligan further explains, as I earlier noted: "What is conventionally called 'crime' is the kind of violence that the legal system calls illegal, and 'punishment' is the kind that it calls legal. But the motives and the goals that underlie both are identical—they both aim to attain justice or revenge for past injuries and injustices."[33] (italics in original).

These human inclinations to justify violent behaviors to effect some change were countered by Jesus. Violence to effect change was not his way. It was not what he expected would grow out of a seedbed of love and prayer. So when disciples James and John, those "Sons of Thunder" (Mark 3:17), were ready to "command fire to come down from heaven and consume" a Samaritan village that had denied them hospitality, Jesus rebuked them (Luke 9:51-56). And when a woman who had been caught in adultery was brought to him, he rejected the violent option of stoning her, even though that was the consequence articulated in the tradition (John 8:3-11). And ultimately, when his own life was at stake, he rejected the violent option of calling down an army of twelve legions of angels from heaven to defend himself (Matthew 26:53).

Yet, Jesus was all about change. And when all else failed, he modeled what he taught. Not willing that even his enemies should perish, he accepted the "other means" of self-suffering as his "engine of change" rather than inflicting suffering on others. In the end, this meant death on a cross by the hands of those who saw him as their enemy.

Later, the Apostle Paul, early church theologian, interpreted Jesus's death as an ultimate act of goodness. As he wrote to the church in the empire capital of Rome, one might actually die for a good person. But an enemy? Paul knew whereof he spoke, for in earlier life he had himself been an enemy of those who followed in the Jesus way. But he saw the believers in Rome, and in all time, as having the same former identity of enemy. And so he wrote: "While we were still enemies, we were reconciled to God through the death of his Son..." (Romans 5:10). Like Joseph of Genesis, who was able to see the larger hand of God in what had happened to him, so Paul was also able to see the larger hand of God in what happened on that fateful day of crucifixion in Jerusalem.

Last Words

Last words of those who are executed are of great interest to those impacted by their prior actions, as well as families and communities who stand by. "Sometimes we remember nothing more than someone's last words," Robert K. Elder notes in beginning *Last Words of the Executed* (2010).

Jesus's last words were also remembered. Even as he was dying the slow death of a cross, his goodness was reflected in last words to family, neighbor and enemy—all three levels of relationships reflected in the fulfillment series of his Sermon on the Mount.

While hanging on the cross, Jesus saw his mother standing nearby close to John, "the disciple whom he loved." To his mother he said: "Woman, here is your son." Turning to John, he said: "Here is your mother" (John 19:26-27). In this final moment of agony, he still engaged in a dance between his family of origin and his family of faith. As the oldest son in the family, he fulfilled his responsibility for his mother by yet providing for her continuing care. From that moment, his aging mother lived in the home of John.

Jesus also had neighbors that fateful day of crucifixion. He was one of three executed. The other two were guilty of unnamed crimes. They, too, hung on crosses, one on each side of Jesus. In an exchange of words, one mocked Jesus challenging him to save himself as well as them, if indeed he was the Messiah. The other, however, rebuked his fellow wrongdoer, acknowledging that both had been justly condemned, but Jesus was innocent. Then turning to Jesus in between, he said: "Jesus, remember me when you come into your kingdom." While silent to the first, to the second Jesus responded: "Truly I tell you, today you will be with me in Paradise" (Luke 23:39-43). As his neighbor on the cross, Jesus honored his request.

Perhaps the most poignant last words of Jesus were reserved for his enemies—those who were executing him: "Father, forgive them; for they do not know what they are doing" (Luke 23:34).

As humans, we tend to stand in awe of those who extend forgiveness to those who have harmed them, sometimes even before being asked. The power of such action is well described by Dag Hammarskjöld, former Secretary-General of the United Nations, in his diary entry for Easter Sunday of 1960. Forgiveness, he wrote, is breaking "the chain of causality because he who 'forgives' you—out of love—takes upon himself the consequences of what *you* have done. Forgiveness, therefore, always entails a sacrifice."[34] As an Easter Sunday entry in his diary, Hammarskjöld poignantly captured what Jesus did as he took upon himself the consequences of his enemies' actions.

Having addressed family, neighbor and enemy, Jesus acknowledged his own physical need. "I am thirsty," he said (John 19:28). And then he expressed a deeper pain as recorded in his mother tongue: "Eli, Eli, lema sabachthani?' that is, 'My God, my God, why have you forsaken me?'" (Matthew 27:46, Mark 15:34). Luke records his very last words as: "Father, into your hands I commend my spirit" (23:46). John records his very last words as simply: "It is finished" (19:30). And as Jesus breathed his last, Matthew, Mark and Luke all report that he ended, not with a whimper, but with a loud cry. Three days later Jesus arose from the dead, as he had said he would.

But Jesus's student-disciples were left with a puzzle. How to make sense of it all? Their nationalistic expectation that as Messiah, Jesus would restore the kingdom to Israel had been dashed. Two of his disciples walking from Jerusalem to the nearby village of Emmaus after his resurrection confessed as much. Jesus had joined them on the way, though they did not recognize him. When Jesus feigned ignorance of recent happenings, his fellow travelers brought him up-to-date on what had transpired in the last days concerning one called Jesus of Nazareth. And then his fellow travelers shared their expectation: "We had hoped that he was the one to redeem Israel" (Luke 24:21).

Jesus, still not recognized, deplored their ignorance of the tradition. He then helped them make sense of what had happened. He called their attention to the tradition of Messiah as suffering servant, interpreting for them, "beginning with Moses and all the prophets," how what had happened fit with this understanding of Messiah (Luke 24:25-27).

Luke's report that Jesus began with Moses in his interpretive journey through the tradition is startling. For it was precisely the Warrior God tradition of Moses and the Exodus that informed his disciples' expectation that the Messiah would again redeem Israel. Indeed, they had just celebrated their annual day of independence from Egypt called Passover, even as nations in our time annually celebrate their days of independence. How could Jesus possibly have found support for a suffering servant Messiah in Moses? We might wish that Luke would have told us more, for even today interpreters struggle to reconcile the Warrior God of Exodus with the God Jesus portrayed in his Sermon on the Mount as one who "causes the sun to rise on good and bad alike, and sends the rain on the innocent and the wicked," and so models unlimited goodness.

Again, though, Jesus did not reject the tradition. Rather, in the pattern of the six fulfillment sayings of the Sermon on the Mount, he saw his death and resurrection as fulfillment of the tradition. And so, beginning with "Moses and all of the prophets," Jesus helped his disciples see in the tradition what heretofore they had not seen and understood.

Jesus confirmed his interpretation of the tradition in a later appearance to his disciples, when he clearly stated: "Thus it is written, that the Messiah is to suffer and to rise from the dead on the third day, and that repentance and forgiveness of sins is to be proclaimed in his name to all nations, beginning from Jerusalem" (Luke 24:46-47).

The family story of Jesus thus ends on a note similar to the final family story of Joseph and his brothers in Genesis. Unearned suffering is a final pathway to redemption. Confession, forgiveness and repentance are its guideposts. This way, furthermore, is to be proclaimed not only to insiders, but to all nations, beginning at home in Jerusalem.

The Space In Between

While the cross represents the ultimate in redemptive suffering, it also occupies what we might call the space in between. The space in between is the space occupied by the reconciler—the one who brings together those who are in tension and conflict with each other. It was the space occupied by Jesus, through whom "God was pleased to reconcile to himself all things, whether on earth or in heaven, by making peace through the blood of his cross," as the Apostle Paul writes in his letter to the Colossians (1:20).

The space in between, moreover, was the space occupied by Jesus when he stood alongside a woman accused of adultery and refused to yield to the judgment of death by stoning. It was the space occupied by Jesus when he dared one day to speak to a Samaritan woman not of his people, who had come to draw water from a village well. It was the space he filled as he stood between his frightened disciples and the raging night storm on the Sea of Galilee. It was the space he filled countless times as he healed the sick, the lame and the blind. It was the space that later Paul and Barnabas filled as they represented outsider Gentile Christians to the Jerusalem Council called to discern their destiny.

Like Jesus, his followers, too, are called to the ministry of reconciliation (2 Corinthians 5:18); that is, to occupy the spaces in between bringing together heaven and earth, on one hand, and brothers and sisters, neighbors and enemies on the other—sometimes simply standing alongside in support of those weak and oppressed; sometimes offering to mediate between those in conflict; and sometimes boldly confronting those who are oppressing others. In the end it may also lead to a cross, as it did for Jesus. But, then, he did say, "take up your cross and follow me." As Dietrich Bonhoeffer has said, "When Christ calls a man [and woman], he bids [them] come and die."[35]

BEST PRACTICE
Love (*agape*)

Love was the cardinal virtue for Jesus at all levels of relationships, including love for enemies. His meaning, however, was that which in the Greek language is called *agape*. Love in this sense is more than sibling or erotic love. A*gape*, moreover, is expressed in concrete behaviors regardless of what one may be feeling. As a best practice, one is hard pressed to define *agape* better than did first century Apostle Paul in his first letter to the church in Corinth. I have formed his behavioral characteristics of *agape*, along with each opposite, into what in English I call an L Scale, L for love. What the Apostle Paul wrote to that first century church in Corinth continues to resonate as a best practice in our time, and so I include it here.

THE L - SCALE : A MEASURE OF HUMAN RELATIONSHIPS

The L-Scale consists of the Apostle Paul's list of *agape* love behaviors in I Corinthians 13 along with their opposites. It is a measure of your relationship with another. You may use it to discern where you stand in relation to another, including whether you are ready to enter into a difficult conversation with another. A low score may suggest that you are not ready; a high score may suggest that you are ready. If high, a positive outcome is more likely.

On each item circle the number that most accurately describes where you are at in relation to another. You may also use the scale to test what you are prepared to commit to as you engage another.

Impatient	1	2	3	4	5	6	7	8	Patient
Unkind	1	2	3	4	5	6	7	8	Kind
Envious	1	2	3	4	5	6	7	8	Accepting
Boastful	1	2	3	4	5	6	7	8	Modest
Conceited	1	2	3	4	5	6	7	8	Humble

Rude	1	2	3	4	5	6	7	8	Courteous
Selfish	1	2	3	4	5	6	7	8	Generous
Irritable	1	2	3	4	5	6	7	8	Self-Controlled
Keep score of wrongs	1	2	3	4	5	6	7	8	Keep no record of wrongs
Gloat over other's wrongs	1	2	3	4	5	6	7	8	Sad about other's wrongs
Sad when truth prevails	1	2	3	4	5	6	7	8	Glad when truth prevails
Slow to excuse	1	2	3	4	5	6	7	8	Quick to excuse
Closed to trusting the other	1	2	3	4	5	6	7	8	Open to trusting the other
Despair of the other	1	2	3	4	5	6	7	8	Hopeful of the other
Give up quickly on the other	1	2	3	4	5	6	7	8	Persevere with the other

_____ My total score (maximum of 120)

(Scores are relative without established norms to indicate degrees of readiness to engage the other. Each, therefore, is left to interpret where they stand in light of the total.)

CONCLUSION

We have journeyed from the ancient world of Genesis to the present in exploring universal pathways to peace. I conclude with a paradigmatic story from my own faith tradition.

Dirk Willems belonged to the radical, Anabaptist branch of the sixteenth century Protestant Reformation. As an adult, he voluntarily chose to follow Jesus, as Anabaptists believed one should. Those so choosing, though baptized as infants into the church of the political region in which they lived, were rebaptized as adults. Their opponents called them Anabaptists, meaning rebaptizers.

In Holland, where Willems lived, Anabaptists were outlawed, with the penalty being death. In the winter of 1569, Willems fled for his life as he was pursued by the local constable. In his way was a stream with thin ice from a recent frost. Though risky, he made it across the ice, but his pursuer broke through and was in danger of drowning. In the Warrior God tradition of the Exodus, Willems might have interpreted his adversary's desperate situation as an intervention of God, as in that earlier Exodus escape God had caused the waters of the Red Sea to overwhelm and drown the pursuing Egyptian army. Willems, however, chose to follow the goodness tradition of Jesus. Seeing his pursuer's life in danger, he "quickly returned and pulled him out of the freezing water, and so saved his life," though in doing so, he imperiled his own.

The constable, now gratefully on the bank of the stream, wanted to let Willems go. But the local village mayor was also present, and "very sternly called to him to consider his oath" of office. Now caught between his responsibility to the office, and his impulse to let Willems go, the constable gave in to authority and arrested him. Willems subsequently experienced "severe imprisonment and great trials." In the end, he was burned at the stake by a "lingering fire."[1]

Stories challenge our imaginations. Stories from sacred texts and faith traditions, moreover, lend authority to what they reveal. Persons of faith are motivated by such stories, yet the interplay between religion and culture has been "almost completely neglected by students of conflict," as noted by rabbi and peace scholar Marc Gopin. "Religion and culture unquestionably play a critical role in numerous conflicts, all the way from intrapersonal to global conflicts," he further observes.[2]

The stories retold in this work point to multiple pathways from no to yes. Negotiation, separations of various varieties, conciliation, reconciliation, and the transformative strategies set forth by Jesus are all possible steps to where peace with justice is at home. And when all of the foregoing fail and one is tempted to revert to violence, there is yet the pathway of unearned suffering modeled by Jesus as a final expression of love for enemies, including oppressors who have chosen violence as their engine of change.

Whereas we stumble toward peace in the present, Jesus's early disciples also saw a future in which God's *shalom* movement would someday be climaxed by new heavens and a new earth. In the vision of the Apostle Peter, "we wait for new heavens and a new earth, where righteousness is at home" (2 Peter 3:13).

So it is that we as humans have a past, a present and a future. The stories from the past capture our imagination as they model ways for living in the present. We seek pathways where "steadfast love and faithfulness will meet; justice (*tsedeq*) and peace (*shalom*) will kiss each other" (Psalm 85:10). And given the long arc of the moral universe, we also anticipate a day when in the vision of the prophet Isaiah,

> "…the wolf will live with the lamb,
> and the leopard lie down with the kid;
> the calf and the young lion will feed together,
> with a little child to tend them" (Isaiah 11:6, REB).

That is our hope!

POSTSCRIPT
Conflict, Violence and Peacemaking Today

Two wars of sufficient magnitude to be called world wars occurred in the first half of the twentieth century. Toward the end of the second, atomic fire like "the radiance of a thousand suns" burst above the Japanese cities of Hiroshima and Nagasaki, ushering in the nuclear age.

Fearing mutual destruction, the "cold war" of the second half of the century followed. Hot regional wars in places like Korea and Vietnam, nevertheless, continued. The century ended with a decade of conflicts ranging from war between nations to internal conflicts between tribal, religious and like groups. It was, indeed, a century of war. More than one hundred million persons died as a result of all these wars, exceeding an average of one million per year. Countless others were injured. Multitudes of still others were displaced as refugees. The beginning of the twenty-first century has been no different.

The first college and university academic programs in peacemaking came into existence in the United States post World War II. Given two world wars, these programs focused primarily on the larger concern of achieving peace among the nations of the world.

My own orientation toward peace at the time, too, was war-oriented. I grew up in Mennonite churches and attended a Mennonite high school. During my senior year in the mid-1950s, I wrote a research paper on "nonresistance" in Anabaptist Mennonite history for a culminating high school class. Turning eighteen in my senior year, I needed to register for the military draft, which was in effect at the time. My research, hence, had considerable personal relevance. Consistent with my church's history and Confession of Faith as a historical peace church, and also personal conviction, I then registered as a conscientious objector to war.

In my Mennonite context this orientation to war came to be known as "the peace position." In a late twentieth-century survey of Mennonites, eighty-one percent of respondents thought their fellow parishioners still viewed "peace and nonresistance primarily as conscientious objection to war."[1] Yet, while I was trying to sort out my own, personal relationship to war in the mid-1950s, other things were brewing around me. And I confess being somewhat oblivious to what was happening. Yet what was developing has led to major growth in our understanding of the breadth of peacemaking.

War, of course, has remained a critical peace challenge. But peace concerns have progressively broadened since the 1950s as new challenges have emerged.

Cultural Change as a Seedbed of Conflict

Norman Shawchuck has suggested that change is the seedbed of conflict.[2] The amount of conflict generated by cultural change during the second half of the twentieth century would seem to validate his claim. Indeed, I suggest that cultural change became the key competitor with war as a foreground peace issue during the second half of the century.

While the military draft and war were still in the foreground for me during the 1950s, something else was happening in the larger culture. Change was in the air.

In 1952, for instance, the United States Supreme Court ruled that movies fall under first amendment free speech protection, opening the door to a much broader expression of sex and violence.

In 1953 television entered the political arena as Dwight D. Eisenhower was inaugurated as president of the United States under the eye of the television camera, but not without competition. On January 19, the day before his inauguration, Lucille Ball gave birth to a baby boy on the same day as her television character, Lucy, gave birth in the series in which she starred. Over sixty-eight percent of the country's television sets were tuned to *I Love Lucy*, competing with the inaugural events. And complementing Lucy and her television family were shows featuring murder and violence. A new television culture was emerging.

Also in 1953, the first issue of *Playboy Magazine* featuring Marilyn Monroe signaled movement toward a sexual revolution. And in yet the same year, the words "women's liberation" appeared for the first time in the United States in a translation of *The Second Sex* by French feminist writer Simone De Beauvoir. Then there was Elvis Presley and the new music of Rock and Roll. And, of course, within time the Beatles.

Here were the seeds of a new politics, the sexual revolution, the women's liberation movement, a new television culture with the likes of Lucy as the new storyteller, and an emerging new music culture.

Then, in 1955, the year I graduated from high school and began my freshman year of college, Rosa Parks refused to give up her bus seat in Montgomery, and the Civil Rights Movement was on.

The cultural changes of the 1950s continued during the 1960s. The decade began with great idealism and promise. In the United States President Kennedy concluded his 1961 inaugural address with a ringing call to service: "Ask not what your country can do for you; ask what you can do for your country." He gave feet to this call by establishing the Peace Corps. In African countries, as elsewhere, independence movements were creating new opportunities and hope.

But the decade soon plunged into confusion and frustration as President Kennedy, to begin with, and then Martin Luther King, Jr. and Robert Kennedy were assassinated. American cities burned as racial tensions exploded. Vietnam became not just a distant war, but a war on the streets of America as the anti-war movement grew. Independence movements in other parts of the world floundered for a variety of reasons.

The Volatile Mix of War and Culture

During the 1960s, the two themes of war and culture came together in a volatile and confusing mix. The mix of the two made it difficult for people, including churches, to discern which of the two they were responding to—war or culture. When men's long hair is mixed with anti-war sentiments, which is the issue? Post-Vietnam, both war and culture have continued as major peace issues, but culture has competed for preeminence.

It is significant that as the second half of the century began, the stage for discourse among Christian thinkers about the issue of culture was set by Richard Niebuhr in his seminal work on *Christ and Culture* (1951). He saw five possibilities: Christ Against Culture, Christ of Culture, Christ Above Culture, Christ and Culture in Paradox, Christ the Transformer of Culture.

Niebuhr placed my own Mennonite people in his category of Christ Against Culture: "The Mennonites have come to represent the attitude most purely, since they not only renounce all participation in politics and refuse to be drawn into military service, but follow their own distinctive customs and regulations in economics and education."[3]

Niebuhr's categorization, while factually true of some Mennonites at that time but surely not all, has rested uneasy with Mennonite thinkers and theologians. So Mennonite thinkers over the past half-century have worked to formulate more accurate and satisfying ways of describing their understanding of the relationship between Christ and culture. More recently, Duane K. Friesen has suggested that "Christ and culture" may be the wrong way of even framing the question. Christ incarnated always implies culture, as he observes, and so perhaps we would do better to speak of alternative visions of culture.[4]

A view of Christ incarnated in cultures that are always complex and keep changing and so keep generating conflicts opens the door to a much larger peacemaking agenda than just war. This larger agenda emerged within time in both the larger society and the church. The seedbed of the post-World War II era with its accelerated cultural and political changes of the 1950s and explosive dynamics of the 1960s led finally in the 1970s and 1980s to new initiatives in peacemaking. Conflict was no longer just a matter of distant wars, as it surely never was. But conflict had come to the main streets of our world with renewed force, and could not be ignored.

Indeed, these main street conflicts found their way into faith communities, including the Christian church. Issues of music and worship styles, women in ministry, sexuality, and the like could not be ignored. Cultural and social change moved to the foreground, and new questions emerged that needed to be engaged.

Innovations in the Seventies and Eighties

The decades of the 1970s and 1980s were a fertile period of innovation. Conflict resolution grew into prominence as a language of peacemaking, followed in time by the alternative expressions of conflict management and conflict transformation. Mediation as an alternative way to resolve conflicts began to grow in popularity. Applications of mediation began to multiply. Peer mediation programs in which children and young people learn to mediate their own conflicts on school grounds began to appear. Community mediation centers emerged in which volunteer mediators from their own communities mediate community conflicts. In the legal field, Alternative Dispute Resolution (ADR) was broadened to new applications.

In my Mennonite circles in the mid-seventies, the Victim-Offender Reconciliation Program was birthed in Ontario, Canada, and Indiana, United States, and has since contributed to a larger restorative justice movement fed by multiple streams, including a return to the ways of traditional cultures. In 1979 Mennonite Conciliation Service came into being, and a decade later International Conciliation Service, both in the larger context of Mennonite Central Committee, the Mennonite world relief and service organization. In 1984 Ron Sider challenged the Mennonite World Conference meeting in Strasbourg, France, to establish "a new, nonviolent peacekeeping force of 100,000 Christians" that could be "sent into the middle of violent conflicts to stand peacefully between warring peoples in Central America, Northern Ireland, Poland, Southern Africa, the Middle East, and

Afghanistan." And Christian Peacemaker Teams came into being, though not yet on the scale that Sider envisioned.

In the larger world, Gandhi's nonviolent approach to social and political change of the first half of the twentieth-century greatly influenced similar movements of the second half of the century, including the American Civil Rights movement and the historic changes in Eastern Europe toward the end of the century, as earlier noted in this work.

Simultaneously, new and expanded academic programs in peace and conflict studies began to emerge in colleges and universities around the world, including graduate programs. The language of conflict resolution (alternatively conflict management and conflict transformation), alternative dispute resolution (ADR), mediation, restorative justice, trauma healing, nonviolent social change and the like have increasingly come to be understood, taught and practiced.

In brief, the accelerated cultural and societal changes of the post-World War II era of the 1950s and 1960s led in the last three decades of the twentieth century to a vastly expanded peace agenda. In some ways, this development was a healthy return to the breadth of the biblical understanding of peace as *shalom*.

Toward century's end, an initial group of twenty-three Christian scholars representing different perspectives and denominations gathered in the United States to again address the issue of war and peace, but with a question viewed as transcending the historic debate between pacifism and just war theory; namely, "What essential steps should be taken to make peace?" Their focus, then, shifted to what they named "just peacemaking," which was proposed as a "new paradigm for the ethics of peace and war." Ten "peacemaking initiatives" emerged out of this collaborative effort.[5] These have been presented as initiatives around which persons of different faiths and theological orientations can unite, and reflect the more activist peacemaking movement of at least the second half of the twentieth century.

Also toward the end of last century, the World Council of Churches chose to begin the new, twenty-first century with a global peace initiative called "The Decade to Overcome Violence: Churches Seeking Reconciliation and Peace"(2001-2010). As the beginning violence of our present century reveals, the challenge remains.

In brief, the movement since World War II has been toward a much broader peace agenda than only war, along with a more activist approach to peacemaking at all levels of life. This work is an expression of that larger breadth and movement. Peace, as in the Hebrew *shalom*, the Arabic *salaam*, and similar words in other languages, has to do with far more than war. Peace is an inclusive word that embraces all of life, symbolized by family, neighbor and enemy.

Note: This "Postscript" is an adaptation of an earlier article appearing in the journal Direction *(Spring, 2003) titled: "Toward a Holistic Understanding of Peace: The Twentieth-Century Journey"*

ENDNOTES
Scripture quotations, unless otherwise noted,
are from the Revised Standard Version of the Bible

Introduction

[1] George Gerbner, "Society's Storyteller: How Television Creates the Myths by Which We Live," *Media & Values* 59-60, Fall 1992, 9.
[2] Phyllis Trible, *God and the Rhetoric of Sexuality* (Philadelphia: Fortress, 1978), 1.
[3] James Gilligan, *Violence: Reflections on a National Epidemic* (New York: Vintage, 1997), 5.
[4] David Brinkley, *Washington Goes to War: The Extraordinary Story of the Transformation of a City and a Nation* (New York: Alfred A. Knopf, 1988), 227.

Chapter One

[1] Erik Barnouw, *Tube of Plenty: The Evolution of American Television*, 2nd rev. ed (New York: Oxford, 1990), 132.
[2] Translation of Robert Alter in *Genesis: Translation and Commentary* (New York: W.W. Norton, 1996).
[3] *Genesis Rabbah*, XXII:VI, as in Jacob Neusner, *The Components of the Rabbinic Documents: From the Whole to the Parts*. Vol. 9, Part 1. *Genesis Rabbah* (Atlanta: Scholars Press, 1997), 209.
[4] James Gilligan, *Violence: Reflections on a National Epidemic* (New York: Vintage, 1997), 110.
[5] John Braithwaite, *Crime, shame and reintegration* (Cambridge: Cambridge University Press, 1989), 55.
[6] Claus Westermann, *Genesis 1-11: A Commentary*, trans. John J. Scullion S.J. (Minneapolis: Augsburg Publishing House, 1984), 304-305.

[7] Mishna Sanhedrin, 4:5; primary parallels in Babylonian Talmud: Tractate Sanhedrin, 37a; and Jerusalem Talmud: Tractate Sanhedrin, 4:9.

[8] Sura 5:32 as in *The Qur'an*, A new translation by M.A.S. Abdel Haleem (Oxford University Press, 2004).

[9] Etienne G. Krug et al, eds., *World report on violence and health* (Geneva: World Health Organization, 2002), 10. See also *Global Status Report on Violence Prevention 2014* available in both hard copy and on the internet at: http://www.who.int/violence_injury_prevention/violence/status_report/2014/en/http://www.who.int/violence_injury_prevention/violence/status_report/2014/en/

[10] Theodore Caplow et al, *The First Measured Century: An Illustrated Guide to Trends in America, 1900-2000* (Washington, D.C.: AEI Press, 2001), 214-215.

[11] Colin Wilson, *A Casebook of Murder* (New York: Cowles, 1969), 25.

[12] *Time*, Dec. 27, 1993.

[13] *Time*, June 29, 1992.

[14] Randolph Roth, *American Homicide* (Cambridge: Belknap, 2009), 3-4.

[15] Ibid., 5.

[16] Thomas Keneally, *Schindler's List: A Novel* (New York: Touchstone, 1993), 48.

[17] Ibid., 368.

[18] William Ian Miller, *Eye for an Eye* (Cambridge: Cambridge University Press, 2006), 20.

[19] Gilligan, 18

[20] Irshad Manji, *The Trouble With Islam Today: A Muslim's Call for Reform in Her Faith* (New York: St. Martin's Griffin, 2003), 42-43.

[21] Alexander B. Downes, *Targeting Civilians in War* (Ithaca and London: Cornell University Press, 2008), 257.

[22] Ibid., 244, 247.

Chapter Two

[1] Stuart Hample and Eric Marshall, *Children's Letters to God* (New York: Workman, 1991).
[2] Albert Bandura, *Social Foundations of Thought and Action: A Social Cognitive Theory* (Englewood Cliffs, New Jersey: Prentice-Hall, 1986), 47.
[3] Alter, 54.
[4] Sir Leonard Wooley, *Abraham: Recent Discoveries and Hebrew Origins* (New York: Charles Scribner's, 1936), 151-152.
[5] John Updike, *Rabbit, Run* (New York: Fawcett Crest, 1960), 44.
[6] Woolley, 153-56.
[7] Elias Chacour, *Blood Brothers* (Grand Rapids, Michigan: Chosen Books, 1984), 60.
[8] Ibid., 137.
[9] Nigel Ashton, *King Hussein of Jordan: A Political Life* (New Haven: Yale University Press, 2008), 5.
[10] Queen Noor, *Leap of Faith: Memoirs of an Unexpected Life* (New York: Miramax Books, 2003), 371.
[11] Avi Shlaim, *Lion of Jordan: The Life of King Hussein in War and Peace* (New York: Alfred A. Knopf, 2008), 575-76.

Chapter 3

[1] Bill Clinton, *My Life* (New York: Alfred A. Knopf, 2004), 542.
[2] Dennis Ross, *The Missing Peace: The Inside Story of the Fight for Middle East Peace* (New York: Farrar, Straus and Giroux, 2004), 119.
[3] Bill Moyers, *Genesis: A Living Conversation* (New York: Doubleday, 1996), 278.
[4] Alter, 187.
[5] Ibid., 187.
[6] Geoffrey Wheatcroft, "Churchill and His Myths," *The New York Review of Books*, May 29, 2008, 8.
[7] Theodore C. Sorensen, *Kennedy*, Perennial Library Edition (New York: Harper and Row, 1988), 717-718.

Chapter 4

¹ Joseph Campbell, *The Power of Myth* (New York: Doubleday, 1988), 22.
² Gilligan, 96.
³ Alter, 190.
⁴ Ibid., 193.
⁵ Samantha Power, *A Problem From Hell": America and the Age of Genocide* (New York: Harper Perennial, 2007), 57.
⁶ Miroslav Volf, *Exclusion & Embrace: A Theological Exploration of Identity, Otherness, and Reconciliation* (Nashville: Abingdon, 1996).

Chapter 5

¹ *The Pioneer*, February 6, 1999.
² Jacob Neusner, *The Components of the Rabbinic Documents: From the Whole to the Parts,* Vol. 9, Part 4, *Genesis Rabbah* (Atlanta, Georgia: Scholars Press, 1997), LXXXIV:VII.2, 73.
³ *Truth and Reconciliation Commission of South Africa Report* (London: Macmillan, New York: Grove's Dictionaries, 1999), 1:104.
⁴ Ibid., 1:116.
⁵ Jacob Neusner, *The Components of the Rabbinic Documents: From the Whole to the Parts.* Vol. 9, Part 6, *Genesis Rabbah* (Atlanta, Georgia: Scholars Press, 1997), 254.
⁶ Alan T. Levenson, *The Story of Joseph: A Journey of Jewish Interpretation* (Williamsburg, Virginia: Dept. of Religious Studies, College of William and Mary, 2004), 104.

Chapter 6

¹ Gilligan, 5.
² Thomas Cleary, *The Wisdom of the Prophet: Sayings of Muhammad* (Boston: Shambhala, 2001), 24.

³Warren S. Kissinger, *The Sermon on the Mount: A History of Interpretation And Bibliography* (Metuchen, N.J.: Scarecrow and The American Theological Library Association, 1975), 6.

⁴Elias Chacour, *We Belong to the Land: The Story of a Palestinian Israeli Who Lives for Peace and Reconciliation* (Notre Dame, Indiana: U. of Notre Dame Press, 2001), 143.

⁵Ibid., 144.

⁶Jaroslav Pelikan, *Divine Rhetoric: The Sermon on the Mount as Message and as Model in Augustine, Chrysostom and Luther* (Crestwood, NY: St. Vladimir's Seminary Press, 2001), 72, 121.

Chapter 7

¹Campbell, 22.

²Ibid., 22.

³Dietrich Bonhoeffer, *The Cost of Discipleship* (New York: Macmillan Paperback Edition, 1963), 143.

⁴Paul Wehr, *Conflict Regulation* (Boulder, Colorado: Westview Press, 1979), 57-60.

⁵Nelson Mandela, *Long Walk to Freedom: The Autobiography of Nelson Mandela* (Boston: Little, Brown and Company, 1994), 22.

⁶*Mishnah Tractate Avot* 3:3.

⁷*Talking About Genesis: A Resource Guide* (New York: Doubleday, 1996), 134.

Chapter 8

¹Lane Cooper, *The Rhetoric of Aristotle* (New York: Appleton-Century-Crofts, 1932), 5.

²*Pirkei Avot* 4.

³M. K. Gandhi, *Non-Violent Resistance* (New York: Schocken, 1961), 42.

⁴Mohandas K. Gandhi, *An Autobiography: The Story of My Experiments With Truth* (Boston: Beacon Press, 1957), 437.

[5] Walter Wink, *The Powers That Be: Theology for a New Millennium* (New York: Doubleday, 1998), 99-100.
[6] Gordon M. Zerbe, *Non-Retaliation in Early Jewish and New Testament Texts: Ethical Themes in Social Contexts* (Sheffield, England: Sheffield Academic Press, 1993), 23.
[7] Wink, 101-103.
[8] Wink, 106.
[9] Miller, 20.
[10] Robert Fulghum, *All I Really Need to Know I Learned in Kindergarten: Uncommon Thoughts on Common Things* (New York: Villard, 1988), 6.
[11] Robert K. Elder, *Last Words of the Executed* (Chicago: The University of Chicago Press, 2010), 246-48.
[12] Howard Zehr, *Changing Lenses: A New Focus for Crime and Justice* (Scottdale, Pa: Herald Press, 1990).

Chapter 9

[1] Volf, 9.
[2] Martin Luther King, Jr., *Strength to Love* (Philadelphia: Fortress Press, 1982), 150-51.
[3] John Howard Yoder, *For the Nations: Essays Public and Evangelical* (Grand Rapids, Michigan: William B. Eerdmans, 1997), 93.
[4] E. Stanley Jones, *A Song of Ascents: a spiritual autobiography* (Nashville: Abingdon, 1968), 136.
[5] Daniel Jonah Goldhagen, *Hitler's Willing Executioners: Ordinary Germans and the Holocaust* (New York: Vintage Books, 1997), 411.
[6] Richard J. Mouw, *Uncommon Decency: Christian Civility in an Uncivil World* (Downers Grove, Illinois: InterVarsity, 1992), 11.
[7] Martin Buber, *Between Man and Man*, trans. Ronald Gregory Smith (New York: Macmillan, 1965), 99.
[8] *Time*, January 3, 1994, 37.
[9] Roger Fisher and William Ury, *Getting to Yes: Negotiating Agreement Without Giving In* (Boston: Houghton Mifflin, 1981).
[10] *Parade Magazine,* September 14, 1997.

¹¹*Testament of Joseph*, 2:68

¹²John E. Toews, *Romans: Believers Church Bible Commentary* (Scottdale, PA: Herald, 2004), 320-21.

¹³Roger Fisher and Scott Brown, *Getting Together: Building Relationships as We Negotiate* (New York: Penguin, 1988), 38.

¹⁴Timothy Garton Ash, "Velvet Revolution-The Future," *The New York Review of Books,* December 3, 2009, 20.

¹⁵Erica Chenoweth and Maria J. Stephan, *Why Civil Resistance Works: The Strategic Logic of Nonviolent Conflict* (New York: Columbia University Press, 2011), 7.

¹⁶John Keegan, *The Face of Battle* (New York: Penguin Books, 1976), 28.

¹⁷Paul D. Hanson, *The People Called: The Growth of Community in the Bible* (San Francisco: Harper & Row, 1986), 241.

¹⁸M.K. Gandhi, *Satyagraha in South Africa* (Ahmedabad 14: Navajivan Publishing House, 1950), 103-107.

¹⁹John Keegan, *War and Our World* (New York: Vintage Books, 2001), 41-42.

²⁰John Keegan, *A History of Warfare* (New York: Vintage Books, 1994), 6.

²¹Ibid., 6

²²E. Stanley Jones, *Mahatma Gandhi: An Interpretation* (New York: Abingdon-Cokesbury, 1948), 88. Note also Chapter 8, "Victory through Suffering," in Stanley Wolpert, *Gandhi's Passion: The Life and Legacy of Mahatma Gandhi* (Oxford, 2001).

²³Clayborne Carson, ed., *The Papers of Martin Luther King, Jr.* (Berkeley: University of California Press, 2000), 4:341-342.

²⁴M.K. Gandhi, *Non-Violent Resistance* (New York: Schocken Books, 1961), 17.

²⁵Alexander Solzhenitsyn, *Lenin in Zurich*, trans. H.T. Willets (New York: Farrar, Straus and Giroux, 1976), 72.

²⁶Wink, 42.

²⁷Volf, 306.

²⁸Wink, 131.

²⁹Fernando Enns and Annette Mosher, eds., *Just Peace: Ecumenical, Intercultural, and Interdisciplinary Perspectives* (Eugene, Oregon: Pickwick, 2013), 41.
³⁰Eberhard Bethge, *Dietrich Bonhoeffer: Man of Vision, Man of Courage* (New York: Harper & Row, 1970), 608-609.
³¹Goldhagen, 418.
³²Enns, 41.
³³Gilligan, 12, 18.
³⁴Dag Hammarskjöld, *Markings* (New York: W.H. Auden, 1964), 197.
³⁵Bonhoeffer, 99.

Conclusion

¹Thieleman J. van Braght, *The Bloody Theater or Martyrs Mirror of the Defenseless Christians* (Scottdale, PA: Mennonite Publishing House, 1951), 741. Trans. Joseph F. Sohm.
²Marc Gopin, *Holy War, Holy Peace: How Religion Can Bring Peace to the Middle East* (Oxford, 2002), 4.

Postscript

¹Leo Driedger and Donald B. Kraybill, *Mennonite Peacemaking: From Quietism to Activism* (Scottdale, PA: Herald, 1994), 214.
²Norman Shawchuck, *How to Manage Conflict in the Church* (Irvine, CA: Spiritual Growth Resources, 1983).
³Richard H. Niebuhr, *Christ and Culture* (New York: Harper, 1951), 56.
⁴Duane K. Friesen, *Artists, Citizens, Philosophers: Seeking the Peace of the City: An Anabaptist Theology of Culture* (Scottdale, PA: Herald, 2000).
⁵Glen H. Stassen, ed., *Just Peacemaking: The New Paradigm for the Ethics of Peace and War* (Cleveland: The Pilgrim Press, 2008).

ABOUT THE AUTHOR

Dalton Reimer is the co-founder and former co-director of the Center for Peacemaking and Conflict Studies at Fresno Pacific University, established in 1990. Earlier, in 1960, he joined the faculty of what was then Pacific College, now University. His first field of teaching was communication, which expanded in later years into peace and conflict studies. He has served the university over the years in various capacities, including nearly two decades in academic administration as dean. Simultaneously, he has served in varied leadership roles in the church, both locally, nationally and internationally. After beginning his journey toward retirement in 2002, Reimer continued his work with the Center for Peacemaking with a particular focus on international peace education development. Along with developing peace educators from a variety of other countries, he has also taught and lectured in institutions of the church and higher education on five different continents. He is the co-editor of *Christian Conflict Resolution*, a reader in the Russian language published in St. Petersburg, as well as contributor to several other works. He is also the author of *The Making of a Distinctive Church College: The Fresno Pacific Model of Becoming 1960-2000* (2020). He earned his bachelor's degree from California State University, Fresno and masters and doctoral degrees from Northwestern University.

www.ingramcontent.com/pod-product-compliance
Lightning Source LLC
Chambersburg PA
CBHW060355080526
44583CB00012B/328